G000229671

# NEXT STOP SEATON!

## 50 years of
## Modern Electric Tramways Limited

The complete and official history of the
Seaton and District Tramway and the
Modern Electric Tramways Company

**BY DAVID JAY AND DAVID VOICE**

**PUBLISHED BY ADAM GORDON**

## ALSO BY DAVID VOICE

**How to Go Tram and Tramway Modelling**
**London's Tramways Their History and How to Model Them**
**What Colour Was That Tram?**
**Tramway Modelling in 'OO' Gauge**
**More Tramway Modelling in 'OO' Gauge**
**The Illustrated History of Kidderminster and Stourport Electric Tramway (with Melvyn Thompson)**
**How to Go Tram and Tramway Modelling, 2nd Edition**
**The Millennium guide to Trams in the British Isles**
**The Definitive Guide to Trams in the British Isles**
**Toy and Model Trams of the World, Volume 1: Toys, Die Casts and Souvenirs (with Gottfried Kuře)**
**Toy and Model Trams of the World, Volume 2: Plastic, White Metal and Brass Models and Kits (with Gottfried Kuře)**

## ABOUT THE AUTHORS

**David Jay**

David's first contact with the trams of Claude Lane was as a child in 1951 when his parents took him on holiday to St Leonards. Coincidentally this was the year that Claude operated his line along the sea front. At his insistence David's parents were persuaded to let David have a ride on the double deck tramcar number 23. A photograph was taken to immortalise the occasion. From that moment David's interest in trams and tramways grew and flowered, though he was to wait 51 years before he got his second opportunity to ride on number 23. He is a member of the Tramway and Light Railway Society.

**David Voice**

David has been interested in trams, both full size and model, for as long as he can remember. His first memory of trams is riding on the London trams as a small child. From reading about the trams of Claude Lane he was deeply interested in them, though he did not get to see or ride on them until they had been moved to Seaton. One of his great pleasures was to see number 23 for the first time at the Large Exhibits Store in Liverpool. A life's desire was fulfilled last year when he was given a ride in number 23. Owing to a difference in scale he was the only passenger in the saloon, but still managed to fill the tramcar. David is the author of many books about tramways and tram modelling; he has also been published extensively in the model railway press. David is the Archivist and Small Scale Modelling Adviser to the Tramway and Light Railway Society.

Copyright: All rights to text and photographs (except where identified) are reserved to David Jay and David Voice. Every care has been taken to ensure the accuracy of the information contained in this publication but no liability can be accepted for any errors or omissions.

A catalogue entry for this book is available from the British Library
ISBN 1 874422 43 5

Publication no. 45

Published in 2003 by Adam Gordon, Kintradwell Farmhouse, Brora, Sutherland, KW9 6LU
Tel: 01408 622660

Printed by The Launton Press, Telford Road, Bicester, Oxfordshire OX26 4LF

Production and design by Trevor Preece: trevor@epic.gb.com

## DEDICATION

**We are honoured to dedicate this book to the late Claude Lane and to Allan Gardner.**

**THE YEAR 2003 SEES THE GOLDEN JUBILEE OF MODERN ELECTRIC TRAMWAYS LIMITED, THE COMPANY ESTABLISHED ON 19th MAY 1953 BY CLAUDE LANE TO RUN HIS TRAMS**

# ACKNOWLEDGEMENTS

We are indebted to everyone at Seaton Tramway for their help in compiling the information for this book. We are particularly grateful for all the time and help that Allan Gardner has given. We spent many a happy hour chatting with Allan and being amazed by his vast reserve of memories. Whenever we compared his memories against written records he was always spot on. It is no exaggeration to say that without Allan's help this book would not have been possible.

We pass our sincere thanks to Sue Gardner for helping with the company records, finding photographs and giving enormous assistance to us. Mark Horner has helped in many ways, not least in sharing his knowledge and experience in the chapter on the operation of the tramway. This is an aspect that is ignored in tramway histories, as most are written long after the end of the system. Seaton Tramway is very much a continuing operation and we are sure that seeing what goes on behind the scenes will interest everyone. Roger Lane kindly checked the work and corrected errors and made valuable suggestions for additional material.

The friendliness of the Seaton Tramway is renowned throughout the tramway world. Our experience has been one of always being made extremely welcome. We have been made welcome on every visit and our most inane questions have always been answered cheerfully.

We also particularly thank Stan Letts. Stan is a volunteer at the tramway. He read our preliminary manuscripts and made excellent suggestions which have made the book much more readable. He also helped to get many of the photographs for the book and wrote the Chapter on his own speciality, the making of transfers for lettering and crests on the trams.

The history of the tramway encompasses a trip from London to the South Coast, then to North Wales, back to the South Coast and then to Devon. To discover information about the tramway we have been helped by an enormous number of people. Everyone has been generous and passed on photographs, information, press cuttings and memories. We thank them all.

Howard Butler
M.G. Colignon
Ted Crawforth
Gordon Dinnage
John Downes
Bill Hands
Daniel Hill
David Holt
David Howard
Ron Howes
Dennis Felton
Gordon Gangloff
Alan Kirkman
Roger Lane
R.F. Mack
Brian Martin
John Meredith
Roger Monk
John Myers
David Padgham
Alan Pearce
Hugh Petrie
Alan Pike
N. Rayfield
W.G.F. Roberts
Graham Sidwell
Mervyn Silk
D. Tate
John Tennent
Rosy Thacker
Geoffrey Tribe
John Twigdon
Brian Wainwright
D.N. Warren
Geoff Wheway
Arthur Whitehouse
Alan Williams
John Wills
Richard Wiseman

Borough of Barnet Archive
Light Rail Transit Association
National Tramway Museum
Tramway and Light Railway Society

We owe profound thanks to our wives and families who gave enormous support and allowed us the space and considerable time to research and write this book.

**PHOTOGRAPHS**

We have done our best to identify the photographer of each photograph and where it is known the name is given. Photographs credited to the Seaton Tramway collection have been taken from the Seaton photographic collection and it was not possible to identify the photographer. If we have used any of your photographs please contact the authors and we will ensure that proper credit is given in future printings of the book.

Huntingdon and Kidderminster
May 2003

# CONTENTS

# INTRODUCTION

The history of Modern Electric Tramways and the Seaton and District Tramway is unique in the annals of British tramways. It is the only tramway to have operated in more than one geographical location. Indeed if the early fête days are called one place, then the tramway has run in no less than five different towns. These moves have not been minor shifts to the town next door, but massive relocations of over hundreds of miles. Each move has been a larger operation than the move before. Now the tramway has purchased its own land in Seaton, so it now has the permanent home that it has sought for many years.

The history of the tramway is also the history of two people. Claude Lane was the driving force behind the building of the first tram and then the wish to operate his own tramway. From the very earliest days he was helped by a young boy, Allan Gardener. Over the years Allan moved from eager volunteer to become Claude's right hand man running the tramways. When the sudden death of Claude made the future of Seaton Tramway uncertain it was Allan who took over the project and realised Claude's vision.

**Claude Lane at his favourite occupation, driving a tram. Here he is at the controls of Blackpool Standard car 99.** *Seaton Tramway collection.*

The book is published in the year of the 50th anniversary of Modern Electric Tramways and soon after the retirement of Allan Gardner as Managing Director of MET and Seaton and District Tramways Company. Amazingly these trams have been carrying passengers longer than many of their full size brothers in British towns. Indeed MET is the oldest commercial tramway company in the British Isles. The Manx Electric Railway is operated by the Manx Government, while the Blackpool Tramway has been municipally operated for most of its life.

While we were writing the book the Seaton Tramway became the visitor attraction of the year 2002-03 for the South West, a prestigious recognition from the Excellence in England Awards. It goes forward to the national ceremony later in the year. A fitting honour for a unique organisation.

# CHAPTER 1

# Claude Lane and Allan Gardner

This book is more than a history of a tramway. It is also the story of two men sharing a common dream and having dogged determination to overcome all obstacles.

The first personality is Claude Willington Lane, who had a vision of operating his own tramway. Little did he realise that bureaucracy would be his greatest challenge. Instead of enjoying running his trams, he found he had to spend valuable time ensuring that his trams had a future. No doubt when he started taking his trams to fêtes he did not realise that over fifty years later his trams would be giving pleasure to thousands of people, young and old alike. Indeed the Seaton Tramway was named as the South West "Visitor Attraction of the Year" for 2002-03.

Our second personality is Allan Gardner, who, from his teenage years, became Claude's right-hand man and who was presented with the challenge of his lifetime upon Claude's sudden and untimely death. Allan's own determination has ensured that Claude's dream did not die with him. It was right and fitting that, in recognition of this dedication, Allan was honoured with the MBE for his contribution to tourism.

So it is only fit and proper that this book starts by introducing the key personalities.

**Claude Lane also drove the streamlined Balloons. Here he is driving car 238, that was originally built as an open top car.** *Seaton Tramway collection.*

## Claude Lane

The story of Modern Electric Tramways, the development of Claude Lane's trams and the making of the Seaton & District Electric Tramway started on 2 June 1908 when Harriett Lane gave birth to her third son at Totteridge, just south of Barnet and near Whetstone, in what was then the County of Middlesex. Harriett and her husband William named their new son Claude Willington Lane, baby brother to Douglas Harvey and Leslie Elworthy.

With his brother Ernest, William Lane was joint Manager of Manor Farm Dairies, Highgate. In the early years of deliveries, milk was taken out in churns and measured into jugs on the doorstep. Later William visited the United States of America where he saw the pasteurisation process with milk being bottled in the dairy. He brought the idea back to his company and before long milk was being delivered in bottles and this soon became the standard way for all dairies to distribute milk. In time Manor Farm Dairies was sold to United Dairies and William became a Director.

**Claude's mother, Harriett.** *Seaton Tramway collection.*

When Claude was three years old the family moved a few miles south to Finchley and nearer to Highgate. His new home was close to the Metropolitan Electric Tramways Finchley Depot (between Rosemont Avenue and Woodberry Grove, just off Ballards Lane). Like all similar families of the time a nanny cared for Claude. He was fascinated by the trams and would persuade his nanny to take him in his push chair to the tram depot so he could watch the trams coming and going. He later described his push chair as a single truck, maximum traction reversed truck type. The maximum traction tram bogie is the type with one axle having large wheels and one axle having small wheels. The reversed type has the small wheels leading. So his push chair had four wheels, the front wheels being smaller than the rear wheels.

Later he discovered that the Metropolitan Electric Tramways had their main workshops at Hendon, not too far from his home. Like all children he would explore the area around his home and one of his favourite trips was to go to Hendon Works and look through the gates at the depot and the workshops beyond. One day he had been staring through them for some time when a man came over and asked if he was interested in the trams. He agreed and to his delight he was invited into the yard and then given a tour of the depot and so was able to see his beloved trams at close quarters.

This was a highlight of his boyhood, though a little while later it was rather tempered when his close friend told him that he had also visited Hendon Works. This friend had been exploring around the premises and found a break in the fence. Squeezing through he had got to the works building, finding a door open he was peeking through when he was caught by the foreman. The foreman realised that it was an interest in trams that had brought the lad in and so rather than ticking him off, the foreman took him on a tour of the works. The lad saw the workshops, watched metal tyres being shrunk onto wheels and the many different machines needed to keep the trams on the road. Claude was always a little envious of his friend's good luck as he never realised this ambition.

### A Flair for Electricity

When he reached school age he joined his elder brother Leslie at Berkhamsted Boarding School. His interest was always towards engineering and electricity. Later he went to a cramming school in readiness for his school leaving certificate. Here the Head was happy to encourage his pupils to develop their personal interests. In the case of Claude it was soon evident that they would both benefit from this approach. The first encounter came when the school generator set, already old and needing refurbishment, became even more erratic. The pupils complained that at night, when they were doing their homework, the light would gradually get dimmer until after an hour or so, it was so faint they could not read or write. The Head suggested to Claude that he might like to have a look and see if he could repair it. Claude soon realised that the problem lay with the supplementary battery. This was charged during the day and would discharge in the evening to provide the extra power needed for all the lights. However, the battery was old and past its lifetime. He stripped the battery and cleaned everything. He found that the lead cells had buckled badly, so he straightened them. He also needed to repair a couple of parts. He approached the Head and asked if he could go to the shops to buy the parts the next morning. Co-incidentally this was a Thursday and the morning lesson was mathematics, Claude's least favourite subject. The Head agreed and Claude missed the lesson, repaired the battery and got the electrical supply to a more acceptable condition, though he did warn the Head that he would soon need to purchase a new battery.

Later the Head purchased a second-hand American car. He mentioned to Claude that it seemed to be a little bit noisy. Claude was happy to have a look and managed to book several Thursday mornings off to repair of the car. The first thing that Claude saw was that when the engine ran it threw out enormous amounts of smoke, as well as sounding awful. Claude decided to look inside the engine and removed the sump. Inside the sump he found large amounts of oil sodden sawdust. The seller of the car had stuffed sawdust into the sump to quieten down the noise of worn out bearings. When Claude inspected the bearings they were completely shot and the sawdust had started to get into lots of other places where it was doing no good at all. Eventually he had no alternative but to tell the Head that he had bought a heap of rubbish. Although this was not good news for the Head he did not blame Claude and they remained friends, particularly when the Head bought a replacement engine and Claude fitted it for him (which meant more Thursday mornings away from classes). At this time Claude was around 15 years old.

### Apprenticeship in Engineering

On leaving school Claude's first job was at the Stoke Newington Electricity Power Station as an indentured apprentice to learn about electrical engineering. He completed his apprenticeship in four years and obtained his Diploma of Faraday House (DFH). He then left the power station and joined Blackstones, a large company manufacturing oil engines at Stamford, Lincolnshire. Here he did an apprenticeship in mechanical engineering, learning how to operate the many machines found in engineering workshops. When he had completed this second apprenticeship he was around 22 years old and he decided to leave Blackstones in order to set up his own business.

He formed the Mobile Welding and Workshop Company based in

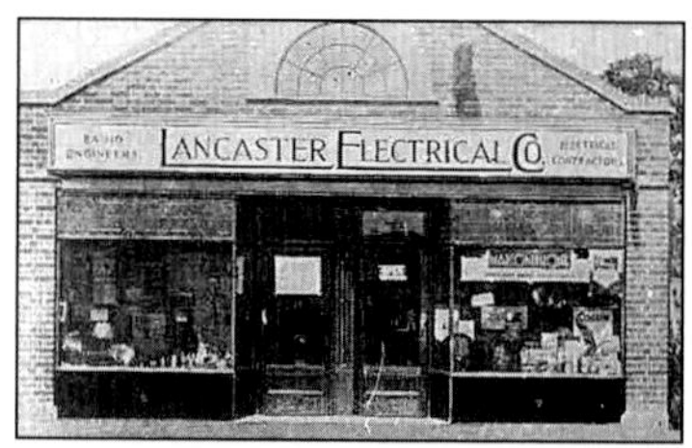


**The Lancaster Electrical Company shop in Barnet.** *Courtesy Barnet Archive.*

Accumulator Service

ELECTRICAL ENGINEERS AND CONTRACTORS

Lancaster Electrical Co.

LANCASTER ROAD, NEW BARNET

Phone: Hillside 2184

**An early advertisement for the company.** *Courtesy Barnet Archive.*

**The small electric bus "Lecar" made for Pinewood Studios.** *Seaton Tramway collection.*

Barnet. This grand sounding organisation was in fact Claude, a friend, a van and some welding gear. They would tour around the many farms then in the area, offering their services to do welding and repairing farm machinery. However, there was not much opportunity to use his electrical engineering skills and he decided to open a small workshop in Lancaster Road, New Barnet. He named it The Lancaster Electrical Company, after the road. Here he specialised in batteries for radios, radio repairs and anything else he could think of associated with batteries. The works were set back off the road and access was by a short driveway. At this time he became an official Dagonite battery stockist. He made a sign that he fitted at the end of the driveway advertising that he stocked Dagonite batteries. This sign was illuminated by battery and he would switch it on at dusk. One evening he switched the sign on and when he looked out it was dark. So he walked up the drive and found the sign switched off. He switched it back on, only to discover later that it had been switched off again. This time when he went down the drive he not only switched the sign on, but he also hid and watched. Sure enough a couple of lads came along and jumped up grabbed the sign and switched it off. The next day Claude went to the local garage and purchased old Ford trembler coils. He knew that he could wire them up to the sign so that they gave a short burst of high voltage (in the way that an electric fence works). He was sure that this would deter anyone from messing about with his sign. From that moment he had no further problems.

**A later advertisement showing another electric vehicle made by the Lancaster Electrical Company.** *Seaton Tramway collection.*

He began to get interested in battery vehicles and larger premises were needed. He found some land in Brookhill Road. This area was known locally as the mud hills from the heaps of spoil that had been dumped there when the Piccadilly line extension to Cockfosters was built in the 1920s and 1930s. Claude purchased some land, which was to become 77-79 Brookhill Road. He had a workshop built on the land and designed it so that it could be extended as and when required.

### Skating and Television

Around this time he got very interested in figure skating and ice dancing. Not only did he enjoy it, he was quite proficient. Over the following years he took his bronze and silver medals for skating. He was training for the gold medal when the war came along and halted his ambitions. After the War he continued to skate for pleasure, but dropped any idea of getting the gold medal. During his ice dancing years he had two partners. The first was Wanda, of whom he was very fond. However, another man came on the scene and Wanda chose to marry him, leaving Claude without a partner for ice dancing. He later joined with Gladys Hogg and had many more enjoyable years of ice dancing. He continued to skate until 1954 when the time commitment at Eastbourne meant sacrificing his skating.

From the mid '30s radio was the major medium for home entertainment. However television was being introduced. Claude had a television set and as part of promoting it he converted one room of his workshop into a small theatre and placed the television on a small stage. Then he invited local people to join him in the evenings and watch television. At the time of the Radio and Television Show at Olympia a local rival firm that was also selling televisions, set up a television in their shop and advertised their own Radio and Television Show. Not to be outdone Claude hired some six-wheel LT type buses from London Transport and advertised free trips to the real Show. He took plenty of people to the Show and generated a large slice of business for himself.

## Tram Driving

He had never lost his love for trams and in 1938 the lure became too great. He wanted to drive trams, but found that London Transport started their tram crew as conductors. He made enquiries and found that he could become a tram driver for the Llandudno and Colwyn Bay Electric Railway. So he went up to North Wales and drove for the LCBER during the summer. He drove part time so that he could also spend time at the Lancaster Electrical works. Unfortunately he had a disagreement with the management and in 1939 he decided to apply to Blackpool for a tram-driving job. Here he was seen by the Traffic Superintendent and after a short interview and a test drive he was given six weeks work. Claude enjoyed this so much that he went to Blackpool to do some driving every season up to 1954.

Upon the outbreak of war in 1939 Claude was pronounced medically unfit for military duties, as he suffered from significant deafness. So he was able to continue his business. This deafness sometimes created problems. People who were not aware of this would think that Claude was snubbing them, or being aloof, because he would not reply when they spoke to him. The truth was that unless he could see their lips he was not aware that they had said anything.

## Wartime Demand for Battery-Electric Vehicles

During the War he joined the Volunteer Fire Crew, on top of his expanding business and his trips to Blackpool to drive trams. The business was doing well because the War meant a severe shortage of petrol, which had to be rationed. Many businesses purchased battery electric vehicles that had no fuel restrictions and could run all the time. Very many of the larger factories were commissioned to do munitions production and small units, like Lancaster Electrical, filled the gap. Over this period the company made many battery vehicles for local deliveries. Claude also developed a new feature for electric vehicles. He linked a three speed gearbox into the drive of the vehicle. This increased the range of the vehicle by 25%. He used a chassis and gearbox from a major vehicle manufacturer. He named the vehicle "Lecar" and the first to be built was a small bus for the Pinewood Film Studios to move staff around their sets.

In 1947 Claude was asked by Blackpool Tramways management to drive the prototype Vambac tramcar

**The "Lecar" chassis showing the gear lever unique to Claude's designs at the time.** *Seaton Tramway collection.*

**Three of the Lancaster Electrical Company's works vehicles outside the shop. This shows both three wheel and four wheel delivery vans.** *Courtesy Barnet Archive.*

number 208, which had been hired by the then Light Railway Transport League for a special trip on 14 September. On the appointed day he turned up for duty and went into the shed to take 208 out. The Rolling Stock Superintendent stopped him and asked what he was doing. When Claude said that the Manager had told him to drive 208 on the special tour he was told that the Manager had asked the Superintendent to make the arrangements and another driver was booked for the duty. Claude was aware that there had been animosity towards him from the regular crews. They felt he was a part time interloper who threatened their livelihood, taking overtime opportunities from them. The relationship that Claude had with the senior management was also resented. Claude did not want to cause problems, either for the management or himself, so he did not argue and walked off.

## "Ok – I'll Build My Own"

He returned to Barnet absolutely seething. On the journey back he decided that he would build his own tramcar and no-one would be able to stop him driving whenever he wanted. The next day he took a stool from the works and sat in front of the shutter doors. He asked one of his men to chalk on the door the outline of his body. Getting up he then announced to his work force that he was going to build a tram and the chalk outline showed the size of the cab. They were used to

**Claude welding the chassis of car 23 in the Barnet workshop.** *Seaton Tramway collection.*

**Claude was used to going to Fêtes. This is a display he took to Barnet Fete in 1931, demonstrating electrical generation and lighting.** *Seaton Tramway collection.*

**Car 23 in primer with Claude trying it out.** *Seaton Tramway collection.*

**Ex-Darwen car 23 at Llandudno with its new number 24.** *TLRS Archive.*

**Painting is coming along well, while some windows have been fitted.** *Seaton Tramway collection.*

**Claude makes final adjustments to the windscreens.** *Seaton Tramway collection.*

unusual projects from Claude, but this one capped all the others. The company employed two office staff, six in the body shop and nine in the engineering shop.

At this time in the LRTL magazine "Modern Tramway" there had been mention of a photograph of a children-carrying British double-deck tramcar that had appeared in a foreign magazine. Whether this had also placed the germ of the idea in Claude's mind it is impossible to say. It transpired that the tram in the photograph was a $^{3}/_{7}$ths scale model of a Huddersfield tramcar that did not run on rails. It was steered at each end and originally was pedal powered. Various motors were tried but none was suitable. The fate of this "tramcar" is not known.

Claude set about designing his tramcar. It was firmly based on the two streamline double-deck trams, numbers 23 and 24 built by the English Electric Company for the 4-foot gauge Darwen system. When the Darwen tramways closed both trams were sold to Llandudno and Colwyn Bay Electric Railway (LCBER) where they were re-gauged to 3 feet 6 inches, retaining their numbers 23 and 24 (though due to a communications error the numbers were swapped when the trams were repainted in LCBER colours). Claude would have been familiar with the design of these trams when he was driving for the LCBER. The design was also quite similar to the streamlined Balloon trams that Claude drove in Blackpool.

The project was to test all the technical experience gained by Claude when building battery electric vehicles. He found, common to many people at the time, wartime shortages were continuing and some parts were difficult to obtain. In particular there were problems getting hold of the curved windows for the front of the tram. These took many months before they were delivered. The tram was completed in April 1949 and test runs were carried out on some track laid in the back yard of the Barnet works. The tramcar was about one-third scale in size. The tram carried a notice proclaiming "This Car Built and Operated by Lancaster Electric Vehicles New Barnet". Strangely it carried Blackpool destinations on its blinds, one saying "Squires Gate & Airport" the other "Bispham". However the tram did on other occasions carry the number "19" and the destination "Barnet". Obviously it could not be fully tested unless it was full of passengers and the local children, informed by the bush telegraph and drawn to the tram as if by a magnet, soon volunteered for a ride in the tramcar.

The track in the factory yard was extended through the works and the terminus was just inside the front gates of the works. The passing public were often astonished to see a tramcar drive out of the factory to the terminus, the driver alight to turn the trolley pole round, then get back into the tram and drive it back into the workshop. The 60-volt supply came from two Blackstone diesel generators.

**Car 23 on a test run in the Barnet factory grounds, with plenty of passengers.** *Seaton Tramway collection.*

**Car 23 in almost finished condition, but taking power from a clip on the overhead.** *Seaton Tramway collection.*

## Allan Gardner

It was at this time that the other major personality in the history of the tramways entered the scene. Allan Gardner, born on 18 April 1937 in Barnet to George and Anne Gardner, the eldest brother to David and Pamela. Allan was another individual who loved trams from an early age. However it was model trains that first attracted Allan to the Lancaster Electrical Company, and as a toddler he would walk past the factory and shop where the window contained lots of radios and radio parts. But even more interesting were some Bassett Lowke Gauge 1 model steam locomotives on display in a glass cabinet at the back of the shop. Then, when the War started, he found that the windows had been painted over and he was unable to see into the shop, until he discovered that he could bend down, peer through the letter-box and still see the locomotives.

As a young boy he went with his family to the centre of London. They took a bus ride to Victoria, where they took the Circle Line. On this first trip on the Circle Line of the Underground, Allan and his brother were excited. They had not been into the centre of London before. In those days the doors of the underground stock were operated by hand. They found themselves in a carriage where the doors on the side away from the platform had been left open. The two boys stood watching the tunnel go past as the train moved. Their father spotted the danger and to their protestations closed the doors. At Westminster station they got out and saw the Houses of Parliament and Big

**Allan Gardner driving car 3 at Rhyl.** *Seaton Tramway collection.*

Ben. Walking towards Westminster Bridge he saw a tram. From that moment on he was hooked on trams, although it was not until later that he had a ride on a tram. On this momentous occasion the family trip was to Woolwich. They went by bus to North Woolwich and then across the Thames on the free ferry. On the other side Allan saw more trams and insisted to his family that they ride back by tram. After appearing not to take notice his father then told him to get on the tram otherwise they would miss it. The trip was not entirely without incident. When getting on the tram Allan's mother had placed the pushchair under the stairs. Later, on a sharp curve, the pushchair shot out of its place, clean off the tram. The conductor gave the emergency stop signal and the tram halted. He then got off to fetch the pushchair and returned with much banter to an embarrassed Mrs Gardner.

On another family visit to the Thames and the Docks they acquiesced to Allan's request to return by tram and trolleybus. This meant a journey through the Kingsway Subway, the first time for Allan. On the way back the tram was lightly loaded and the driver noticed Allan staring intently at him. Calling back to the conductor to shut the saloon door, the driver opened his door and spent the rest of the journey chatting to Allan.

## Claude and Allan Meet

During Allan's school years he would walk past the Lancaster works, occasionally spotting a battery vehicle being wheeled out and moved around. This continued until one day, when Allan was eleven years old, he got a real surprise and saw a tram outside the front of the workshop. Stopping in wonder, Allan was so fascinated by the tram that he forgot about not tres-

**Allan Gardner at Eastbourne.** *Seaton Tramway collection.*

passing on private property and he stepped from the pavement to the yard. Absorbed as he was, he did not notice a man come over until a loud voice said "What are you doing?" Allan replied that he was admiring the tramcar. The man was Claude himself and he soon recognised that Allan was truly interested in trams. Allan told Claude that his father and uncle had lived in Nottingham when they were boys and told him of the times they would ride on the open balcony of the trams, with bags of winkles, eating the contents and throwing the shells at pedestrians below.

At home Allan excitedly told his mother and brother about the tram. The next day he took his brother to see the tram, but his brother never had the same interest as Allan. On a later visit Allan heard the men discussing taking the tram to the Uxbridge fête. Allan had already done some Saturday work on a milk round and bread round. So he suggested that he could help them by working for them at the fête. To his delight they agreed and asked him to come over early Saturday morning. His first job was to drive the tram up a ramp on to the trailer. Claude would clip a long lead to the trolley pole and connect the tramlines forming the ramp to the lines in the yard. This allowed the tram to be driven on the ramp, saving much heaving and manhandling. At the fêtes the line consisted of a single track terminus leading to a turning circle. Allan was the "points boy" at the turning circle. He would also nip up to the terminus to turn the trolley pole while the driver and conductor sold tickets, as well as other odd jobs. But it was the setting up and taking down that really interested Allan.

**Allan Gardner (seated) and Paul Anderson taking a break from driving and conducting at Eastbourne.** *Seaton Tramway collection.*

**Car 2 leaving the Eastbourne depot with Claude Lane at the controls.** *Photograph John Wills.*

# CHAPTER 2

# Fêtes, Garden Parties and St Leonards

News about the tram soon got around Barnet and Claude found himself being asked to take his tram to local fêtes and garden parties. Initially he had to decline the invitations. Trams need to run on rails and the only suitable rails were permanently set in the factory yard. However this was a challenge that he could not resist and soon he developed some portable lengths of track and an overhead wire and poles that could easily be put up and taken down. The rails were made from steel channel with steel angle forming the continuous checkrail. The channel and angle were welded to steel pads, which were then screwed to wooden sleepers. The overhead bracket arm traction poles were made from steel tubing welded to a length of channel. A further piece of channel was welded at right angles and the pole supported by bracing strips. The pole fitted in place by sliding the main channel under the rails, the cross channel rested on the tops of the sleepers. This made a very firm support. The power supply was to come from the batteries in the electric lorry (type JR2 built at the Lancaster Works, registration number HJH 370) that took the equipment to the sites. He was now ready to take his tram to a larger audience.

On the 2 July 1949 he took his tram, track and overhead to the Hadley House Conservative Fête. The tram proved a resounding success. It was more popular than any other attraction at the fête, drawing long queues for a ride on the little tram. His next outing was on 23 July at South Mimms, when the tram was filmed by British Movietone News. The word spread very quickly and Claude found himself at the receiving end of many requests to take his tram out. So almost every summer weekend would find him out and about, going to events as far away as Hitchin and Uxbridge. Indeed photographs of the tramcar in operation appeared in newpapers in the USA and Australia.

BARNET DIVISION CONSERVATIVE ASSOCIATION

HADLEY HOUSE

FETE

HADLEY HOUSE HADLEY GREEN

(by kind permission of Mr. and Mrs. A. W. Stone)

This Saturday, 2nd July

2.30—10 p.m.

*Peter Robinson's* Mannequin Parade

Giant MAT Slide

DOG SHOW

*The Hogarth* PUPPETS

Entry Forms for Dog Show from Miss Mitchell, "Cintra," Tudor Road, New Barnet. Barnet 0024.

*First showing at any Fair in the world*

MODEL TRAM

GIVING RIDES TO CHILDREN

INTERESTING ENJOYABLE UNIQUE

MODEL Aeroplane FLYING

Welwyn Garden City Keep-Fit Girls

HILLIAN Juvenile Cabaret

Presented by Miss Lillian Baker

Admission 1/- (before day 9d.); Children 6d.; from Cowings Library, Barnet.

**The advertisement in the local paper for the Hadley House Fête and the first appearance of the trams.** *Courtesy Barnet Archive.*

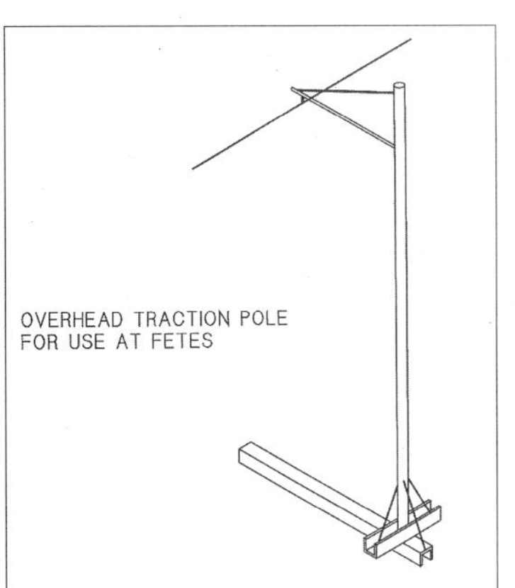


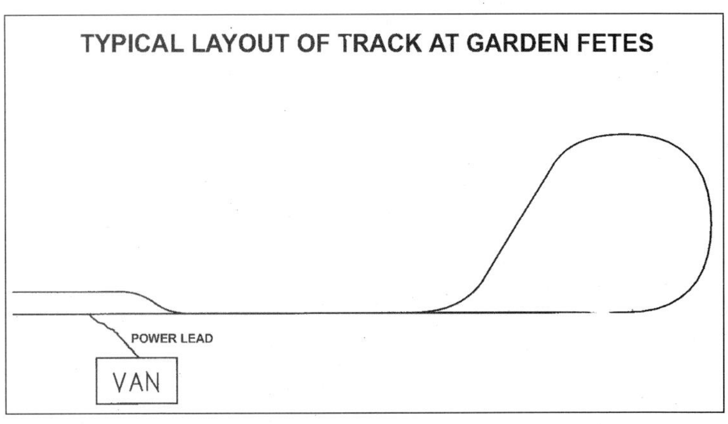

**The portable track designed by Claude that was taken to the Fêtes.** *Photograph authors.*

**This is believed to have been taken at the first Hadley House fête.** *Seaton Tramway collection.*

A pattern was soon established for such events. A lorry would go out to the event the evening before, taking the track, poles and overhead. These would be set up ready for the fête the next day. On the day itself the lorry and trailer would take the tram and batteries. The tram would be run all day and in the evening everything was packed up, as much as possible put on the lorry and taken back to the works. The following day the lorry would go out and pick up the remainder.

Not everyone appreciated the popularity of the trams. There was one occasion when the children formed long queues for a tram ride. Nearby the operator of fairground swings, Bruno Tagg, a local antique dealer in New Barnet, was upset because his rides were getting very little attention or business. By mid afternoon he got fed up and decided to pack his rides away. In the course of packing up he managed to reverse his lorry over the tram track, pulling down the overhead and breaking a couple of traction poles. Claude quickly put the broken poles on to the lorry and took them back to the works in order to repair them by welding. But by the time the journey to and from the works was made with the time taken to weld up the poles, the best of the afternoon had gone and their takings had suffered badly.

The worst fête was that at the Territorial Army. The field that was to be used was the one they did their training exercises on. It was a very rough field and before the tram track could be laid they had to get some shovels and level off the surface. It was hard work and they were not very pleased. Another bad day was at South Mimms. It rained hard the day before the fête and the whole of the actual day. To round off an appalling weekend the lorry and trailer got bogged down in the field and had to be towed off by a tractor. Worse was to come when they went to Hitchin. In those days Hitchin was a long journey. Having set up the track the evening before and taken the tram all was ready for the day. The Mayor arrived and just before he was due to open the fête there was a cloudburst, soaking everything. This then turned to a regular downpour for the rest of the day. The fête was washed out completely and at 4.30pm they packed up everything, without having carried any passengers. To round off the day the trailer tyre got a puncture, deflated and caught fire. They managed to drive to a pub and left the trailer on the car park with a note saying it would be moved the next day. One can imagine the reaction of the landlord peering out of his window in the morning and seeing a tram in his car park. By the time they got back it was too late for Allan to travel home. So he stayed at Claude's house. Allan was extremely worried because he

**Car 23 at the first fête.** *Seaton Tramway collection.*

could not let his parents know what was happening, as few people had phones in their homes at this time. When he got back the next day they understood and he did not get into the trouble he had expected.

In addition to assisting at fêtes, Allan would help in the workshop during his school holidays. The workmen would allow him to develop his engineering skill by letting him practice on the machines and even do some welding. He was also taken out to help in the collection of various sub-contracted items. This included trips to the West Midlands when chassis frames were collected from the Darlaston works of Rubery Owen.

Demand for rides on the tram always outstripped the number of passengers that could be taken in the little tram, leading to long queues. So Claude decided to build another tramcar. Looking back to his days as a tram driver in Blackpool he chose the distinctive 'Boat' design (officially known as the 'Luxury Toastracks'). This choice was no doubt influenced by the ability of the Boat design to carry adults more easily. Built to the same 15-inch gauge the new tram was completed in 1950 and was given the number 225. It went to its first fête in May.

At this time small vehicle manufacturers like The Lancaster Electrical Company were beginning to suffer from greater competition from the larger international automobile manufacturers. The big factories had recovered from the war effort and were now gearing themselves to supply affordable motor cars to the general public. The specialist small factory, particularly with battery driven vehicles, was bound to suffer. Indeed by the 1960s the only battery-powered vehicles in any numbers were milk floats, where the constant stop-start journeys suited this type of traction.

At one time there was an additional problem for them. The works were broken into for each of three weekends. It was a strange situation because while things were moved around the workshops nothing was taken. Claude decided he would set a burglar trap. Between two of the workshops was a short passage with a sump hole. This acted as a drain in wet weather and was invariably full of dirty, oily and greasy water. Claude covered the hole with some planks, just tacking them together so that anyone stepping on them would fall into the sump. He warned all the workers to avoid the planks. On the Monday morning they came in to work to find that there had been no break in over the weekend. They

**An early photograph of car 23 at a fête.** *Seaton Tramway collection.*

**Cars 23 and 225 at a later fête at the stub end terminus.** *Seaton Tramway collection.*

**Car 225 at the TA fête, showing the rough ground.** *Seaton Tramway collection.*

thought no more about it. Later Peter Cresswell called in at the works dressed in his naval uniform. He knocked at the door and Claude shouted for him to come in. Of course he came across the planks and immediately disappeared. Allan saw his naval cap floating on the water and Peter spluttering to get out of the sump. They pulled him out and he said he would be in real trouble for damaging his uniform. So Claude had to phone Portsmouth and explain what had happened to prevent Peter from getting in trouble.

**Car 23 at Uxbridge Agricultural Show in 1949 with the Lancastrian Electrical Company van HJH 370.** *Seaton Tramway collection.*

## A Permanent Site – The Search is On

The idea of running his own tramway became even more attractive to Claude. During the winter of 1950-51 he decided to see if he could have a more permanent site that would have large enough numbers of visitors to keep the tramway busy. He went out at weekends with Lionel Boylett to search for a suitable site. They finally got a good reception at St Leonards, Hastings. During 1947-48 there had been a short 10¼-inch gauge miniature railway on the beach at St Leonards. So they were used to railed transport. The site selected for the tramway was from the Bathing Pool to Marina, with a small depot by the Bathing Pool. The proposal was debated by the Council. While the Baths and Foreshore Committee recommended letting the site to Claude, there were some objections. Some residents felt that they would be disturbed by the noise of the trams, while others complained that the environment would be spoiled by the seven-foot high poles and overhead wires. The Council decided to over-rule the objections and grant the letting for one year.

**Mayor to Open Model Tram Line at Marina**

HERE are seen two model passenger-carrying trams which will soon be running on the promenade at Marina, St. Leonards, from the Bathing Pool to a point opposite the eastern end of Grosvenor Gardens.

The first tram will be driven by the Mayor, Alderman J. D. Cooper, on Whit-Saturday.

The trams, a single-decker carrying eight passengers and a double-decker carrying 14 passengers, were made by Mr. C. W. Lane, who is a tram enthusiast. They are said to be the smallest of their kind in the world, but have a maximum speed of 12 m.p.h. and electric brakes. They are operated by an overhead wire and a trolley arm.

Fare will be threepence single and sixpence return.

**The announcement in the local Hastings paper that Claude's trams were to come to St Leonards.** *Courtesy Hastings and St Leonards Observer.*

Claude purchased new rails and traction poles (using old boiler tubes from ships). All the material delivery and track-laying was done at the weekends. Once the track and overhead was ready Claude took down tram number 23. He had just bought a new Morris J type van. In those days new vehicles

**Cars 23 and 226 well patronised at the terminus.** *Seaton Tramway collection.*

**A view of much of the line from the Marina terminus.** *Seaton Tramway collection.*

were hard to come by and when one was available that was what you got. So the colour was not the one Claude wanted, but to get the van he accepted what was available. Having managed to get it, he then wanted to run it in himself, as he thought his employees would not be careful enough. So he drove it down to St Leonards with the tram on the trailer. When they arrived the sea was pounding the shore and splashing over the track. The crew retreated to the depot for shelter, then to the caravan to sleep overnight. The next morning was completely different, with a clear sky and the sun shining.

## St Leonards Gets a Tramway – For a While

The 15-inch gauge track was laid as a straight stretch of single track alongside the road, with a small depot at one end, with a stub siding at the passenger stop, and a double spur terminus at the other. The line was around 200 yards long and the depot was an existing small building alongside the bathing pool. The building was too low to take number 23, so the roof had to be raised. The power supply came from a set of batteries that was charged from the mains using a vehicle charger. The track came from a mixture of the original portable track taken to fêtes (including the points) and new track constructed from proper 14 lb per yard light flat bottom rail spiked to wooden sleepers. One end of the overhead wire was fixed to the tram depot. Claude had difficulty with the other end. The tension was too much for the usual traction pole. However, close to the terminus was a Council bus shelter. So he ran the overhead wire to the shelter and fixed it firmly. This lasted for the whole of the operation of the tramway and no one ever realised that Claude never had permission to use the shelter.

The track layout allowed one tram to be loaded while the other was on its journey. The trams carried the destinations "Bathing Pool" and "Marina". The line opened at 2.30pm on Whit Saturday, 12 May 1951 by the Mayor Alderman J.D. Cooper. The trams were reported as having a top sped of 12mph. The fare was threepence single and sixpence return, while Claude paid the Council £100 for the concession, with the promise of a further £50 if the venture was a success. Allan helped out when he could. This was usually at weekends and during the summer school holiday. The reaction of the public was the same as when the trams ran at fêtes. Whilst everyone enjoyed his or her ride on the trams, one frequent comment was "why haven't you got an old fashioned tram?" The streamlined appearances of both the Llandudno car and the Boat were too modern for the average customer. So in the winter of 1951-52 Claude constructed his third tramcar, now numbered 3. This was a traditional

**The Bathing Pool terminus with car 225 in the depot and car 23 on service.** *Seaton Tramway collection.*

**Car 23 on service on a colder day.** *Photograph authors.*

British design open top four-wheel tramcar with no windscreen for the driver. The passengers could have the delight of riding in the open air on a sunny day and if it was wet they could keep dry in the lower saloon.

It was not always sunny at St Leonards. At times the weather could be distinctly bracing, with a cold, rain-specked wind having an unimpeded journey across the beach to the tramway. Claude was often surprised to find hardy families queuing up for a ride, with their overcoats on and umbrellas protecting them from the rain and afterwards saying how much they had enjoyed the ride.

**Car 225 driven by Allan Gardner with his brother as passenger (left), on a cold windy day.** *Photograph John Meredith.*

## The Battle of Hastings

However everything was not always so welcome. There were often complaints from the manager, Mr Newton-Moss, of the Wilton Hotel, which was located the other side of the road from the tramway. He would be seen in the evening watching the tramway, checking that it stopped running and the trams were put away by 9.00pm in accordance with the letting conditions. If a tram was still running at 10 minutes to 9.00pm he would call to the driver that he had only ten minutes left to run the tram. He complained to Claude that the noise of the trams was disturbing his guests and the vibration was making the cups and saucers rattle on the tables! The matter came to a head when a group of blind children arrived one evening. The leader asked if it was possible for them to ride the tram. Claude readily agreed and waived all charges. They were given several trips up and down the line and thoroughly enjoyed themselves. As the children left, the hotel manager arrived complaining that they were running past 9.00pm. Claude told him that he was the most miserable person he had ever had the misplеasure to meet and that he had just given rides to blind children who had good reason to be sad, but who were among the happiest people he had ever met. So the manager was to go away and stop bothering them. This was the last occasion that the hotel manager complained about late running.

But such a slight is not easily forgotten and in July formal complaints were put to the Council Committee. A petition signed by 41 people was submitted and some local people attended in person. So when, at the end of the season, Claude met Council members to discuss a letting agreement for the next year the Council referred to the complaint. The members looked embarrassed and said that they were not able to extend the letting because they had many objections to the tramway. When news got out a petition signed by 100 people supporting the tramway was given to the council. Alderman J.D. Cooper (yes the man who drove the first tram) spoke out in support, but the final decision was not to extend the letting.

It was then necessary to remove everything. So more weekends were spent dismantling the track and overhead and transporting it

**A very young David Jay on his first ride in 23.** *Photograph authors.*

**Cars 23 and 225 waiting for passengers at the Bathing Pool terminus.** *Seaton Tramway collection.*

**About half way down the line with car 23 and just one passenger.** *Seaton Tramway collection.*

**The Marina terminus with cars 23 and 225 collecting passengers.** *Seaton Tramway collection.*

**This gives a good indication of the size of car 23, with mothers placing their children into the car for a ride along the front.** *Seaton Tramway collection.*

**Marina terminus with Claude standing to the left of car 23.** *Photograph John Meredith.*

back to Barnet. Having taken back the trams and the overhead they went back to fetch the track, only to find it had disappeared. A local resident told them that a Council lorry had removed it. So they found the Council depot and looked around. There were no employees around, but they found the track in one of the buildings. They loaded their lorry and drove off, still not having seen anyone. Ever one to play a prank, Claude wrote to the Council asking where his track had gone!

There is a postscript to the St Leonards part of the story. The Council Committee were very aware that the tramway had increased visitors to the town and had benefited business for the other attractions nearby. So in December the Council Committee were reported to be recommending a new site for the tramway immediately to the south of the Boating Pool, at the Fishmarket and to offer Claude Lane a seven year agreement. However, the suggested new site was next to an existing miniature railway and Claude did not want to compete against it. In any case it was too late, the tramway had been moved back to Barnet and agreements reached elsewhere for the 1952 season.

**A good view of car 23.** *Photograph John Meredith.*

# CHAPTER 3

# Voryd Park, Rhyl

A friend of Claude, George Clark, who was from Rhos on Sea and who worked for the Llandudno and Colwyn Bay Electric Railway, knew of Claude's difficulties and was looking around to see if there was any suitable site that the tramway could move to. Quite local to him, at Rhyl, was the Voryd Park amusement centre. Located opposite the Marine Park, the amusement centre was a permanent fair ground with a number of rides and other entertainment for visitors. In the years prior to Claude's arrival it had a miniature railway which had fallen into disuse, possibly due to the more famous, rival 15 inch miniature railway running around the lake in Marine Park. The Marine Park railway had been established by the renowned miniature railway specialists Wenman Bassett-Lowke and Henry Greenly. The line was opened in 1911 and ran until 1969 when it closed and the track lifted. In 1978 the line reopened with new track. There was a further temporary closure between 1985 and 1987 while a new owner was sought.

When Claude went to Rhyl to inspect the site and discuss terms with the Twigdon family, owners of the fairground, the Marine Park miniature railway was not only well established, but also famous among model engineers. It could well have created animosity to have two rival 15-inch gauge rail attractions so close together. In fact the relationship between the two organisations was always very amicable and they supported each other as much as possible.

The grounds of Voryd Park were originally part of the gardens belonging to Voryd Hall. In the 1930s Voryd Hall grounds were used as a holiday camp site, with old motorbuses used for accommodation. The site was requisitioned during the War and the Hall was demolished. After the War, in 1944, Arthur "Sonny" Twigdon purchased the site, intending to create an amusement park. The Twigdon family had a long history of fairground amusements and general haulage. At the same time as acquiring the site they purchased Sheringdon House, a large three storey detached house on Quay Street facing the amusement park. This became the family home.

The Voryd Park site was set between Wellington Road and the Promenade. The west boundary was Quay Street. The first fair opened on a small patch of land alongside Quay Street as the Army were still requisitioning the main field. After the cessation of the War the larger field was available and the fair moved on to it, while the original area became a coach park. The boundary on the east was alongside the Alhambra (later renamed the Ritz). Rhyl Amusements acquired

**The Voryd Park fairground was built on the grounds of Voryd Hall after its demolition. In its latter years the Hall was used as a camping ground for holiday visitors.** *Photograph John Twigdon collection.*

**A view of the fairground showing the big wheel, the photograph was taken after the tramway had left.** *Photograph John Twigdon collection.*

the rest of the land towards Sydenham Avenue and built more fairground attractions. They also owned the much larger amusement park across Wellington Road by the Marine Lake.

The Twigdon family built a typical fair ground, with a big wheel, dodgem cars, electric speedway cars, electric motor boats and side shows. A younger children's ride, the Peter Pan Railway, was built on the old foundations of

**The fairground from the big wheel, taken after the tramway had left.** *Photograph John Twigdon collection.*

Voryd Hall. From the start the family did not own all the attractions. They would agree concessions or even lease out some of the rides. To encourage visitors to return each year new attractions were added, replacing the less profitable rides.

What Claude found at Voryd Park was an abandoned small railway with the locomotive gently rotting away as the weeds grew up around it. This was the remains of the "Lilliput Railway". It had a 60-yard end to end run with an unusual gauge of 11¼ inches. The motive power was a Caledonian 4-4-0, number 769 built by D. Croall around 1900. The railway started running around 1948 and ceased around 1950. The engine is now in Glasgow Transport Museum. It was strange to find a true scale model to an unusual gauge working in a fairground and it attracted many model engineers.

**The railway that was replaced by the tramway. Its owner and driver was Len Bealand.** *Photograph John Twigdon collection.*

## The Move to Rhyl

Claude's discussions with the Twigdon family went well and it was agreed that they would lease land for the tram line for the 1952 and 1953 seasons. A depot was built and the track, traction poles and overhead were taken from Barnet for re-erection at Rhyl. Allan, then fifteen years old and in his last year at school, was commissioned by Claude to construct the tramway. He went up to Rhyl for the Easter holiday and laid the track and constructed the depot, which had been prefabricated in the Barnet works. He also went there during the long summer holiday to finish the setting up and run the tramway for the season. The St Leonards track was used, which combined the original track and points built for use at fêtes with the 14 lb per yard flat-bottom rail spiked to wooden sleepers. The route was around a quarter of a mile long. From a double track terminus by Wellington Road, it ran on single track parallel to the road to the entrance to the Park, using the fête track. There was a tight right angle turn leading the track towards the sea, finishing by the big wheel with another double track terminus. The two road depot, capable of taking four trams, was near the corner at the Wellington Road entrance. It was a timber framed building with a corrugated metal cladding. All the track was ballasted railway fashion except at the entrances to the park where paving was laid flush with the rail top to allow easy access for pedestrians and a road for coaches. A continuous check rail was laid on the tight curve.

Taking advantage of his former connections with the neighbouring Llandudno & Colwyn Bay Electric Railway, Claude acquired the services of that company's linesmen. Using their own elderly Morris Commercial tower wagon they soon had the overhead equipment in place. There was a tense moment when George Clark, the head linesman, found that the

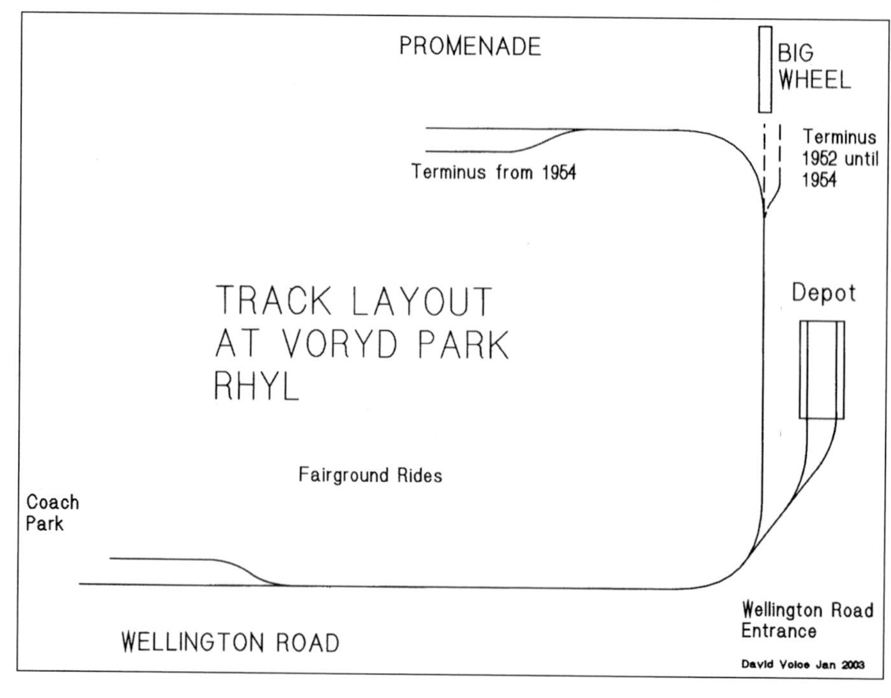

**London Transport car 179, the tram that Claude Lane nearly purchased.** *Photograph Richard Wiseman.*

tension of the wire was too much for the end straining pole. But this was soon rectified and the overhead completed. For power Claude used the same supply that the Twigdons had for the other attractions. Two old Manchester buses were fitted with generators and used as a power station. Claude installed batteries in one of the buses and connected them to the rails and overhead to provide the 60-volt electrical supply. The feed lines went from the top of the bus to the nearest traction pole, the positive connected directly to the running wire with the negative going down the pole to the rail. Like the original portable tramways the power was taken to the trams via an overhead wire. Each tram had a trolley pole with a swivel head that collected the current.

There was another tramway connection in the Park. The big wheel was regulated through a controller from a former Manchester tramcar. Apparently it was the habit of the big wheel operator to grease the gear wheels while the ride was in use. So he would dab chunks of grease over the drive gears as the wheel picked up passengers. Of course when the wheel was full it would be driven around at top speed, while specks of dirty grease were spattered everywhere.

## A London Interlude

In 1952 the London tramway system was being closed. Since taking over the capital's public transport London Transport had been systematically running down and removing trams from the street and replacing them with buses. The programme of closures was interrupted by the War, when having a means of transport not reliant on imported fuel was very useful. But as soon as the War ended the replacement programme was implemented. The last day of tramway operation was 5th July 1952. Previously some trams had been sold to Leeds and one to Sunderland. But the remainder were destined for scrap. London Transport did keep two trams for historic purposes, later adding a third when the Leeds system closed. In 1952 tram enthusiasts were seeking to preserve more examples. Peter Davis purchased number 1858 and after some adventures, including a spell in Chessington Zoo, the tram can be seen running at the East Anglia Transport Museum. Claude Lane also made an attempt to save a tramcar, number 179. But full size trams take up an enormous amount of room. Peter Davis was having difficulties finding storage space for 1858 and Claude could not find anywhere for 179. So the proposed preservation failed and the tram became the last tram to be burnt at the scrap yard in Penhall Road, on 29th January 1953. However, Claude did purchase the gongs from 179 and they were fitted to his number 2, where they remain to this day.

## Rhyl Operations Begin

Trams 23 and 226 were moved up to Rhyl and the tramway opened at Whitsun Bank Holiday weekend for the 1952 season. Allan found accommodation for the summer season at Rhos-on-Sea and spent the whole of his time working on the tramway. He

**Car 23 picking up passengers at the Coach Park terminus.** *Seaton Tramway collection.*

**The depot with cars 3 and 225 getting ready for the day's work.** *Photograph Brian Martin.*

**Car 23 at the Coach Park terminus, the house in the background was owned by the Twigdon family.** *Seaton Tramway collection.*

**At Barnet car 3 is nearly ready to make its trip to Rhyl.** *Seaton Tramway collection.*

had the unusual experience of starting each day's journey by riding on the L&CBER line to Colwyn Bay on the first leg of his journey to Rhyl in order to drive the trams.

The very encouraging reception from the public was, perhaps, a little surprising because of Rhyl's closeness to Colwyn Bay, where they could see and ride on a real tramway all along the coast to the holiday resort of Llandudno. It was a popular tramway with enthusiasts, but it was reaching its final years. In the mid-1930s it had supplemented its own ageing fleet with second-hand single deck cars from Accrington and ten open top double deck cars from Bournemouth. These open top cars proved to be the mainstay of the line until its closure. After the War two streamlined double deck cars numbers 23 and 24 were acquired from Darwen. These were the trams that gave Claude his inspiration for his first tram, which he also numbered "23". But the post war decline continued and the Llandudno and Colwyn Bay line finally closed in March 1956.

While at Rhyl the trams had destination blinds reading "Depot", "Reserved", "Promenade" and "Wellington Road", though later "Sea Front" replaced "Promenade" on number 23. The fares were 4d single and 6d return. The tramway was a great success. However, being surrounded by fairground rides, the public viewed it as just another of the amusement park attractions. Being squeezed in amongst the other rides meant that the total length was limited and a little artificial, as the track curved round and the two termini were only a short walk apart. Following the comments from the public at St Leonards, Claude wanted to add a tramcar that was much more like a traditional British open top tramcar. He saw a photograph of a Portsdown and Horndean four

**Allan Gardner with car 225 at the Coach Park terminus.** *Photograph D Tate.*

**Car 3 at the Wellington Road entrance looking towards the depot.** *Seaton Tramway collection.*

window 'Preston' style open top tram. It was just the sort of tram he wanted. He used the design as a basis and the Barnet works built a tramcar to that style, but not as a proper copy. It was given the number 3 because it was not based on any particular prototype and because it was the third tram to be built by Claude. The new tramcar was completed in June 1952 and taken to Rhyl on the back of the works lorry. It arrived very early in the morning, much to Allan's relief as he had a sleepless night awaiting its arrival. Several L&CBER tram drivers were on their way to work and stopped amazed at such a small tramcar. This little open-top four-wheel tramcar proved very popular. However it was soon realised that it was really too small to meet the peak demands (indeed all passenger tramcars built since have been bogie cars).

During the first summer Allan stayed at 81 Penryhn Avenue, close to the L&CBER depot. The meals were prepared by Miss Whittaker and much appreciated by Allan. He remembers with relish the wonderful Lancashire Hot Pot that she would prepare. She would look at Allan's spindly frame, at the time he weighed nine stone (57 kilos), and say, "Look here young man you need fattening up, I'll see to that!". Sadly she died at the end of 1952 having contracted cancer.

On the Rhyl tramway Allan had a salutary experience one day. It was a miserable wet day with very few people around. Allan let the other driver take time off to go shopping. After a long wait with number 23 at Wellington Road terminus a lady arrived with a child for a tram ride. As an adult she had to sit in the lower saloon, with her baby. Allan drove them round to the terminus by the Big Wheel. Then he set off for the return trip. He was coasting downhill when suddenly found that the tram started slowing as if the rheostatic brake had been operated. He checked his controls, but it was still at "Off". Puzzled he looked around but could not see anything wrong. Then the tram started to lean and slowly it toppled on to its side. Allan checked that the lady and baby were not hurt. They were confused but otherwise fine. He found he could not get

**Car 225 by the Twigdon roundabout.** *Seaton Tramway collection.*

**Note the stop on the end of the track is just a row of loose bricks!** *Seaton Tramway collection.*

out of his driving position because the driver's cab door was now against the ground. So he opened the door to the saloon and helped the passenger open the central door and climb out of the vehicle. The two Twigden brothers saw what had happened and rushed over. Seeing that no one was hurt and the tram empty they started working out what to do. First they suggested switching off the power. One went over to the bus to find that the tramway batteries had been lifted off their shelf and were hanging halfway up the stairs. Allan then discovered what had happened. The trolley pole had dewired, but because the tram was coasting and there were then no dewiring indicators, he had not realised what had happened. The pole had swung away from the bracket arm traction poles so there was nothing that it could hit, until it reached the overhead feed wire. On impact the wire wrapped itself around the trolley pole. The tram dragged the wire, lifting the batteries which slowed the tram down. Then the tension pulled the tram over, but the weight of the batteries meant it fell slowly. The Twigden brothers, two very large men, went to the tram and lifted it back up and on to the rails. To everyone's amazement the tram was undamaged, even the glass in the windows had not broken. Allan drove it back to the depot and checked it over, but it did not need any work and it went back into service.

## An Underground Tram for the RAF

News of the trams in Rhyl had somehow reached the Air Ministry who, in 1952, approached the Lancaster Electrical Company to build a battery operated, single deck, four wheel, 2ft gauge tramcar. Apparently such a tramcar was needed for a top secret underground installation, actually a munitions store at Hertford Hill,

**Car 23 at the Promenade terminus, by the big wheel, this being after the Twigdons had taken over running the tramway. They extended the track round to the Peter Pan railway.** *Seaton Tramway collection.*

Derbyshire. It appeared that the tram would act as a passenger and goods carrier, though it was also to be equipped with provisions for taking a stretcher, for use in case of accidents. Claude Lane agreed that they could make the tramcar and so the Air Ministry placed the order. Claude had expected this to be a small order easily completed. So a start was made.

Claude realised that Allan would be called up to serve his National Service around the same time as the tramcar would be ready. The plan was to have the tramcar ready at the same time as Allan went into the services. Claude then would inform the Air Ministry that they had the ideal person to commission and maintain the tramcar, so Allan would spend his service in Britain. Unfortunately the Air Ministry changed the specifications and delayed the construction of the tramcar. The major change being that the controllers had to be fire-proof. With all these delays on the part of the Air Ministry, the vehicle was still unfinished by the time the company had moved on to Eastbourne. Here a little more work was done on the tram. However the Air Ministry closed the special store and cancelled the order for the tram, which was taken into the Eastbourne works fleet.

In Rhyl the tramway prepared for the 1953 season. The trams were taken back to Barnet for maintenance and refurbishment. In the Spring of 1953 the track and overhead were checked and repaired. So the tramway opened for another season with Claude and George Clark running it. By this time Allan was sixteen and had decided that he would be wise to develop a proper career, as he doubted that he could make a career of operating small trams (how wrong subsequent events proved these doubts to be!). He joined the London Underground as a signal box boy, working at Finchley

**Car 225 with Claude Lane at the controls.** *Seaton Tramway collection.*

Central Signal Cabin. The work involved shift operation. Allan would finish on Saturday at 1.00pm and go straight to Euston to catch the 2.05pm train north. He arrived in Rhyl at 9.15pm that night. After a night's sleep he would work on the tramway all day Sunday, then in the evening catch the train back to London, arriving at 4.00am. He would make his way to the underground station, which was closed. He waited for it to open and would go down to the platform and snooze until the first High Barnet train arrived. At High Barnet station he would catch a bus to take him home. He went to bed to catch up a little more sleep and then would report to his job for the start of his 2.00pm – 10.00pm shift.

Because he had gone to Rhyl straight from work he was still wearing his uniform, including his peaked cap. On one trip home he got on the bus and made his way to the seat behind the driver. The bus had started

**A rare photograph of number 6 in its original condition. It did not stay long at Rhyl.** *Photograph Brian Martin.*

**Car 3 in service at Voryd Park, by the Coach park terminus.** *Seaton Tramway collection.*

very promising. But one Trustee had doubts and vetoed the arrangement. So the proposals came to nothing.

It was beginning to look as if the offer by Captain Howey would be the only possibility, when late one Sunday Claude stopped at a petrol station on the Eastbourne coast in order to get back to London. He peered into the darkness and asked the attendant what was along the road. The attendant said that it was the Crumbles (a beach and firing range). Claude thought that this merited further investigation and decided to go back the following Saturday.

Given the experiences at St Leonards, Claude was not sure about either the proposed site or the likely reaction of the Council, and discussed his apprehension with Allan. Allan suggested that they write to the Council, which would only cost 1½d and the worst that could happen is either being ignored or a downright refusal. So in May Claude wrote to the Council who passed the matter to their Entertainments and Pleasure Grounds Committee. They decided that the appropriate Officers of the Council should look into the request in more detail. So, to Claude's surprise, the Lancaster Electric Company received an invitation to demonstrate the tramway before the Council's officers. A date was booked in September and track and trams 3 and 225 were transported back from Rhyl to the South Coast, reminding everyone of the old fête days.

off when he flopped into his seat. As he did so the bus bell rang and the driver did an emergency stop. Allan then realised that as he sat down the peak of his cap had caught on the bell pull wire and given the emergency stop signal. The driver looked round to see what the problem was and Allan waved an apology indicating that his cap had rung the bell. With a laugh the driver carried on his way.

On 19 May 1953 Claude set up Modern Electric Tramways Limited, a separate company from Lancaster Electrical Company, the purpose being to create a holding company to own and operate the tramway, no matter where it was. The origins of the name come from the first tram, number 23. Claude had painted a fleet name on the side and had used "Modern Tramways". He took those words and realised that if he put the word Electric in the middle the initials would become "MET", the same as his beloved Metropolitan Electric Tramways, the company that built the tramways in North London. Thus Modern Electric Tramways came into being and now celebrates its Golden Jubilee. It was the holding company for the Eastbourne Tramways and now for the Seaton and District Tramways.

## A New Site – The Search Begins Again

Claude was not satisfied with the tramway at Rhyl and at the end of the 1953 season he started looking again for a more suitable site. Starting at Great Yarmouth, he spent each weekend touring around seaside towns, gradually moving south and ending up on the south coast. He had contact with Captain Howey at the Romney, Hythe and Dymchurch Railway, who offered to allow the trams to run on his railway if they used batteries and only on the section without any overbridges. However, a site was found near Folkestone where Claude found some suitable land. Negotiations started with the Trustee owners and everything was

## The Choice is Eastbourne

The demonstration was set up for 17 and 18 September 1953. Various senior Council officers came down to see the trams running and have a ride on them. Among them was George Hill and he fell in love with the trams. He promoted the proposal and the Council gave approval in principle. Learning from the St Leonards experience Claude ensured that the arrangement was for more than one season and on 13 November 1953 the Committee agreed to a five year concession to Modern Electric Tramways to run the tramway, from 1 April 1954 to 31 March 1959. Permission was also given to erect a depot building 40 feet long and 13 feet 6 inches wide and 35 traction poles set 20 yards apart. In January 1954 Claude made an application to the Committee to extend the agreement for a further five years, but this extension was not agreed by the Committee, which only confirmed the initial five year period.

In order to meet the start date, track had to be laid very quickly. Every weekend the lorry would go from Barnet to Eastbourne with track and equipment. In the Barnet factory a great deal of preparatory work was

**Cars 6 and 23 at the Promenade terminus.** *Photograph Brian Martin.*

undertaken. Allan welded roof trusses from metal sections. Concrete was mixed and blocks and pillars cast ready for transport by lorry to the Eastbourne depot. The first section of tramway at Eastbourne commenced operations on 4 July 1954.

Meanwhile, back in Rhyl the tramway was still running, but was no longer operated by Modern Electric Tramways Limited. Claude had realised that building and then operating the Eastbourne line would take up all his available time. So he reached an agreement with the Twigden family. They would take on a lease to run the Rhyl tramway that Modern Electric Tramways Limited would continue to maintain. Trams 225 and 3 were removed from Rhyl, going back to Barnet for refurbishment and then on to Eastbourne. This left just tramcar 23 at Rhyl.

## Tramcar Number 6

Claude felt that this may not be sufficient to meet the demands of the public and so in the winter of 1953/54 he very quickly built another tramcar in the Barnet works. Numbered 6, this was built to a cross-bench, or "toastrack" design which is about the bare minimum that can carry passengers. The chassis has a floor on which there is crossbench seating. There is a small dash panel at each end, with controllers and brake handle. In the centre is a trolley standard, holding the trolley pole high in the air, so it can reach the overhead.

When no. 6 arrived at Rhyl, it did not get the enthusiastic response Claude had hoped for. The Twigdens looked at the toastrack and said that it looked too much like trams running "down the road". These were the LCBER's own toastrack cars which were popular with visitors on hot sunny days. They said they were not going to pay extra for that tram (they did not seem to realise that the big sisters of number 23 were also

**The lack of passengers on an obviously busy day and the shine on 3's paintwork all suggest that the tram has just arrived and is on trial before going into service.** *Seaton Tramway collection.*

**Car 23 at the promenade curve. This shows the tram near to the end of the life of the line at Rhyl. Note the cab door has been removed to make access to the cab easier and lights have been added around the roof. This photograph was the first time that Allan had seen that 23 had been illuminated.** *Photograph John Twigdon.*

running on the LCBER). Claude realised he needed to satisfy the situation and said that they could have number 6 for no extra cost. Even then it proved unpopular with the Twigdens and was returned to Claude in the same year, being taken back to the Barnet works.

The Twigdens ran the tramway from 1954 to the end of the 1957 season. They made some changes to the tramway. One modification made soon after taking on the running of the tramway was to extend the northern terminus by adding a sharp turn by the Big Wheel and laying track to a new terminus alongside Peter Pan's Railway. Later they fitted lights around the edge of the roof and along the trolley pole, to turn 23 into an illuminated tram. The original agreement ran out in 1957 and Claude realised that the success of Eastbourne was taking all his time and effort. It was impossible to continue to have the responsibility of travelling to Rhyl and maintaining the track and trams, particularly when they were being driven by people who were not tram enthusiasts. Inevitably the trams were given a hard ride and needed more maintenance than when Allan was looking after them. One example is that the cab doors of number 23 were removed to make it easier for the driver to nip in and out of the cab. So the tramway at Voryd Park, Rhyl was closed and the trams and track removed to Eastbourne. Also at this time the Twigdon family were arranging the sale of the amusement park to the Butterworth family and the transaction went through soon after the 1957 season.

Down the road, in Colwyn Bay, the Llandudno and Colwyn Bay Electric Railway (L&CBER) had closed one year earlier, on the 24 March 1956, after operating for 49 years. The company that ran the Rhyl tramway, Modern Electric Tramways (MET), was set up in 1953. Today, fifty years later MET is still running tramways, now in Seaton. So the small company has had a longer life than the L&CBER.

# CHAPTER 4

# The Eastbourne Era, 1954-1969

The seaside town of Eastbourne, in East Sussex, faces roughly southeast on to the English Channel. It has acquired a reputation for Victorian gentility, making it a much favoured holiday resort. Eastbourne is also significant to transport historians, as in 1903 it became the first town in the country to run its own municipal motor omnibuses.

At the north-eastern extremity of the town's shoreline the seashore widens into a somewhat wilder stretch of sand and shingle, known as The Crumbles, with Langney Point jutting out into the sea. It is this part of Eastbourne that is the scene for the next fifteen years of our history of Modern Electric Tramways Limited.

## 1954 – The Move and a Change of Gauge

Claude decided that the new tramway at Eastbourne would be laid to a gauge of 2 feet – increased from the former 15 inches. With the exception of the diminutive number 23, all the other tramcars could be regauged without too much problem. The wider gauge would also allow larger tramcars to be built. It meant that new track was needed, but the old track was not available anyway, as it was still needed in Rhyl where operations were still continuing.

A five year concession had been granted for the tramway to run in Princes Park, from the Gates to Wartling Road, where a depot was to be built. Initial track laying at Eastbourne started in March 1954. Construction of the track was similar to that used at Rhyl. Flat bottom rail was laid on wooden sleepers. All the joints were bonded to ensure a good electrical contact for the return current. More overhead traction poles were required and again old marine boiler tubes were purchased. It must be remembered that at this time the country was still feeling the effects of the wartime effort and there were still shortages of materials. So the ex-marine boiler tubes were very welcome. They also found that the accumulation of lime scale over the outside of the tubes gave extra protection against the ravages of the salty atmosphere.

In these early post-war years paint was another scarce commodity. Claude noticed an advertisement in *Exchange and Mart* for some cheap ex-ministry green paint, and enough was purchased to paint all the poles. When it arrived it was found to be spirit-based and when hand-painted it would blow off the brush in fine lines, sticking like a spider's web to everything around,

**Car 3 having been regauged runs by the depot in the early days of the Eastbourne tramway.** *Photograph John Meredith.*

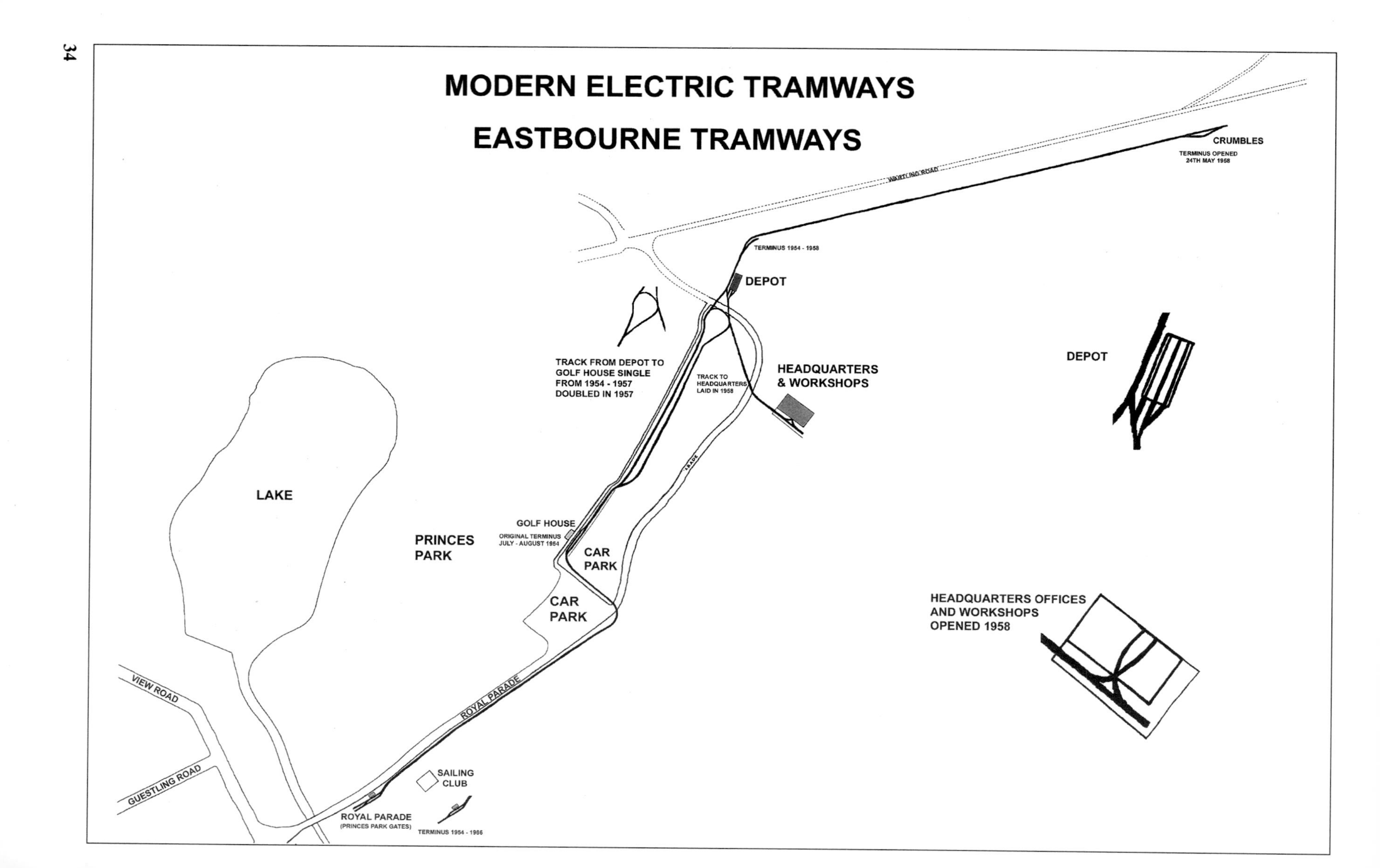

MODERN ELECTRIC TRAMWAYS
EASTBOURNE TRAMWAYS
CRUMBLES
TERMINUS OPENED 24TH MAY 1958
TERMINUS 1954 - 1958
DEPOT
DEPOT
TRACK FROM DEPOT TO GOLF HOUSE SINGLE FROM 1954 - 1957 DOUBLED IN 1957
TRACK TO HEADQUARTERS LAID IN 1958
HEADQUARTERS & WORKSHOPS
LAKE
GOLF HOUSE
ORIGINAL TERMINUS JULY - AUGUST 1954
PRINCES PARK
CAR PARK
CAR PARK
HEADQUARTERS OFFICES AND WORKSHOPS OPENED 1958
VIEW ROAD
ROYAL PARADE
GUESTLING ROAD
SAILING CLUB
ROYAL PARADE
(PRINCES PARK GATES)
TERMINUS 1954 - 1966

**Car 226 under construction at Barnet for use at Eastbourne.** *Seaton Tramway collection.*

**Laying track at the depot, by the look of it on a very warm day. Note the flat wagon used to carry sleepers and other heavy items.** *Seaton Tramway collection.*

particularly the clothes and faces of the painters!

At the same time as all this work was going on in Eastbourne the Barnet factory was busy preparing the tramcars and making parts for the depot building. Tramcars numbers 3 and 225 were transferred from Rhyl to Barnet and the running-gear rebuilt to the wider gauge. While all this was happening the new toastrack tramcar number 6 was being built for Rhyl. With essential maintenance also being done for the Rhyl tramway this was an extremely busy time for everyone.

By Sunday 4 July 1954, 230 yards of track had been laid from the depot to the Golf House and the first passenger-carrying trams began running. The electrical equipment was not modified, so the line voltage was kept at 60 volts, stepped down from the mains, with a diesel generator kept in reserve for emergency supplies. From the start of the project Claude had decided that tramcars numbers 3 and 225 would not be sufficient to run the tramway. So work commenced on two new tramcars. The first was another open boat tramcar to become number 226. It was built to a similar design to number 225, but was made two inches wider. The second was number 238 and was based on the Blackpool "Balloon" design. Externally it looked like a double deck tramcar, but inside the upper deck floor had been omitted except for short sections at each end over the driver's cab. These were reached by small staircases and reserved for children.

Work continued on the last part of the approved line from the depot to Princes Park Gates. This section opened to the public on 15 August 1954. The new tramcar number 226 was ready by this time and it was used on the new section of line. The reaction of the holiday makers at Eastbourne soon showed it to be a good location. The small tramway was very popular. A turning loop was planned for the terminus near the depot, which would speed up operations. The tramway was given the title, "Modern Electric Tramways Ltd., Eastbourne Section" (alluding to the other operation still running in Rhyl).

## 1955 – The First Full Year

The Council had agreed to the erection of a shelter and sales kiosk at the Princes Park terminus and a small shed for an emergency generator. The tramway opened at Whitsun with an official civic opening. The Mayor of Eastbourne was invited to officiate, which he did by driving number 226 the full length of the line, other local officials riding as passengers. A reception was

**Another view of car 3, note the temporary overhead.** *Photograph Ron Howes.*

**Cars 3 and 225 at the depot in the early days.** *Seaton Tramway collection.*

**Another early photograph with only two roads laid into the depot shed.** *Seaton Tramway collection.*

held in the depot, appropriate speeches made, and the party boarded number 226 again to be taken back to Princes Park Gates. Welcome publicity was given to the event by the BBC, who filmed the opening and broadcast it on two occasions over the next few days. A cameraman rode on number 225, which drove ahead of the official tram, so that a good view was had of the Mayor driving the tram.

On 23 July 1955 number 238 (the "Balloon") went into service. The special feature of this tram was that its open interior allowed some additional standing passengers to be carried above the normal seating capacity. This was very helpful in moving the crowds on busy days. Often trams would fill at Princes Park Gates and when they got to the Depot terminus no one would want to alight. Number 238 was able to pick up passengers and reduce waiting time at the Depot.

**Cars 3 and 226 at a temporary Park Gates terminus.** *Photograph W. G. F. Roberts.*

The fare structure in 1955 was:

| | Royal Parade | Crumbles |
|---|---|---|
| **Golf House** | 1½d | 1½d |
| **Crumbles (Depot)** | 3d | |

A return ticket was 6d and there was also a "Park & Ride" ticket for 6d.

1955 was a good season and Claude decided that a new, even larger, tram was needed to cater for the public. He realised that it would be necessary to design an entirely new type of tramcar, made specifically to meet the needs of the Eastbourne Tramway.

It will be recalled from the previous Chapter that the open toastrack number 6 had been rejected by the Fairground operators at Rhyl, and had been returned to

**Car 3 at the Depot terminus in the very early days.** *Seaton Tramway collection.*

**Car 226 under the control of a young driver.** *Seaton Tramway collection.*

**Car 238 at Park Gates terminus, showing children on the upper end platforms.** *Seaton Tramway collection.*

**Car 3 between the depot and the Golf House before the overhead has been erected.** *Seaton Tramway collection.*

**Car 238 waiting for passengers at Park Gates terminus.** *Seaton Tramway collection.*

the Barnet works. Here the chassis frame was adapted for the new tramcar. The design had a large open top upper deck area with 180° reverse stairs at each end. The real innovation came with the lower deck. Instead of an enclosed saloon, the downstairs seating was made in a cross-bench arrangement with access through six openings each side, similar to the 4-wheel open top, cross bench lower deck trams that used to run in Lytham St Annes. The upper deck seats came from a real Bournemouth tramcar and so were adult size. Altogether the new car could seat 40 passengers, double the capacity of number 3. Work commenced on the tramcar (which was to retain its number 6) in 1955, and the re-building work progressed during the winter of 1955/56.

## Allan gets His Call-Up Papers

Allan was still working for London Underground and travelling to Eastbourne on his days off in order to help with the running of the tramway. He was now liable for his National Service, but because the scheme for a small works tram for the Air Ministry had fallen through there were to be no "special arrangements" for him. He duly received his call up papers and on 25 September 1955 he enlisted at RAF Cardington. After his eight weeks' basic training at West Kirby on the Wirral he was posted to Oldenburg, in Northern Germany. The base had Hunter jets and 14 Squadron Venom Vampires. Then in January 1957 he was moved to RAF Schleswigland and worked at Brekendorf radar site, the only hill for miles around. When on the rotating scanner it was possible to see as far as the Danish border, the Baltic Sea, the North Sea and Hamburg. Allan continued his tramway interest. He purchased a cheap second-hand Opal Kapitan saloon car and used it to visit towns and cities with tramways, including Hamburg and Kiel. Of course, he kept in touch with the Eastbourne tramway and visited it on any possible occasion.

**3d ticket used during the early days of the tramway.** *Courtesy David Padgham.*

**Adult 6d ticket, the first type to be used.** *Courtesy David Padgham.*

## 1956 – Crumbles Extension Planned

In January Claude made application to the Entertainments and Pleasure Grounds Committee to build a 330 yard extension to the Crumbles. Permission was refused, so Claude made arrangements to attend the next meeting of the Committee. This was on 17 February 1956 and the Committee were swayed by the case put by Claude. So permission in principle was given. But on 20 April this was amended to formal approval for a 320-yard extension. At the same meeting the five year agreement was extended by a further season and now gave the concession to 31 October 1960. Then at the meeting of the Committee on 19 October 1956 the Committee agreed to a further extension of the concession for another three years, so the agreement now extended to 31 October 1963. The line was secure for the short-term future.

The 1956 season was celebrated with the Mayor of Eastbourne re-opening the tramway on the Whit Weekend Saturday. Boat Car 226 was given an overall

**Car 6 approaching Parks Gates on a busy day, judging by the number of parked cars.** *Photograph Geoff Tribe.*

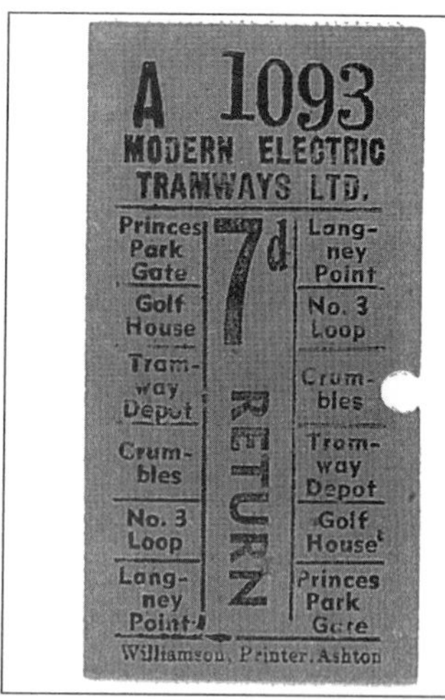


**After the extension to Langney Point a new ticket was used – this is the 7d adult return.** *Courtesy David Padgham.*

**Car 6 at the depot.** *Seaton Tramway collection.*

decoration for the occasion. The BBC televised the opening and the film was included in "Children's Newsreel" on Sunday 27 May.

The fare structure in 1956 was:

| | Royal Parade | Crumbles (Depot) |
|---|---|---|
| **Golf House** | 3d | 3d |
| **Crumbles (Depot)** | 4d | |

A return ticket was 7d.

There were now five trams running at Eastbourne, cars 3, 6, 225, 226 and 238. Throughout the year the tramway was very busy. As well as operating the Eastbourne Tramway the Company had been undertaking the maintenance and repairs to the tramway at Rhyl. This was getting too much for the company, so agreement was reached with the owners of Voryd Park that the Rhyl tramway would run one more season and close in the autumn of 1957.

Around this time number 226 was getting to the end of its passenger life and it entered the workshops to be stripped down to become the first works car number 01. The body was taken off the chassis except for the two dashes that were left in place. A trolley standard was fitted in the centre of the flat deck and a crane was fixed to the floor. It was painted an overall dark grey. In appearance it looked very much like the American flat-bed works cars that many of their trolley systems had. The tramcar was used to move heavy equipment and parts around the system.

In December 1956 an application was made to the Entertainments and Pleasure Grounds Committee to double the track between the Golf House and the depot in order to improve the operation of the tramway. Permission was granted and work started at once. Track laying was also in progress on the Crumbles extension.

**Parts of the tramway could be rather bleak. Car 225 approaching the curve leading to the Golf House.** *Seaton Tramway collection.*

## Road Developments – A New Conflict

The year had started with a meeting of the Committee on 18 January.

**Works car 01, formerly car 226, in its first guise parked outside the workshops.** *Seaton Tramway collection.*

**The trolley reverser at Park gates terminus in action.** *Seaton Tramway collection.*

**Works car 01 and the lorry (a converted bus) outside the workshops.** *Seaton Tramway collection.*

They informed the company that they proposed to extend Royal Parade to link with Wartling Road. The new road would need to cross the present tramway twice. The company agreed to relay track along the seaward side of the new road as and when construction started. They also pointed out that the road would isolate the present depot building and therefore requested permission to construct a new depot and repair works about 320 yards east of the present one. The repair works could be commenced as soon as the plans were approved, but the new depot would not be built until it was necessary to vacate the old one. Drawings of the new building were submitted in February. It was to be 100 feet long and 40 feet wide and would include a tram shop, garage, traffic office, engine room and model railway exhibition. Permission was granted on condition that it was used only for the purposes of the Tramway and that any income from the exhibitions was subject to the same percentage payment as revenue from the tramway. As it turned out the building was never used as a shop or for exhibitions.

## Problems with the Extension

At the same time the tramway was given a severe shock. A representative from the Chatsworth Estates called and asked why new tram track was being laid to the Crumbles. Claude replied that it was the extension approved by the Council, to which the representative said that the Council had no right to do that as it was on land belonging to the Chatsworth Estates which had been gifted to the Council with restrictions. Obviously work on the extension halted while the issue was sorted out. The biggest problem appeared to be that the Council had failed to consult with Chatsworth Estates about the matter. The land had been given to the Council by the Marquess of Huntingdon in 1926, but subject to certain conditions.

After great deliberation and consultation with legal experts it was found that the tramway was on council land, but close to the border with the Chatsworth Estate who, as they had not been informed, now put in an official objection. After many meetings and proposals a compromise was reached, the objection would be withdrawn

**Car 7 at the Crumbles terminus.** *Photograph John Meredith.*

provided the line of the tramway was moved fifteen yards away from the Chatsworth Estates boundary. Everyone was happy about this except Claude. The track had already been put down and now it had to be lifted and moved across fifteen yards. All this effort seemed to have very little point, other than to satisfy the ego of the Estates management. At the same time the new building was discussed and agreement reached about its construction.

### 1957 – Allan Returns to "Civvy Street"

Allan returned to England in September 1957 and Claude loaned him his Hillman Minx to drive to RAF Innsworth, between Gloucester and Cheltenham, for his "demob". Having some spare time he took a walk in the countryside towards Cheltenham. To his surprise he discovered the remains of an open top tramcar in an orchard. It still had one seat on the top deck. He often wonders if this was the remains of Cheltenham 21, which was saved in 1961 and restored before moving to the National Tramway Museum, Crich. It is now in store in Cheltenham waiting to be displayed in the town.

On leaving the RAF Allan was in a dilemma. Should he return to the Underground or work full time for Claude on the Eastbourne Tramway? He chose the Tramway and informed his manager at the Underground. He was told that if things did not work out he could always go back to the Underground, where a job would be waiting for him. Thus reassured he contacted Claude feeling that it was not quite the risk that he had imagined. He worked at Eastbourne over the winter, assisting in the relaying of the track.

### 1958 – The Crumbles is Reached

The additional work in lifting the track that had already been laid and moving it fifteen yards to the side meant that the opening of the extension was delayed until 24 May 1958. Claude took the opportunity of making use of the battery-operated four-wheel car built for the aborted Air Ministry scheme that was converted for overhead operation, given the number 02

**Allan Gardner (seated) and Paul Anderson at Princess Park Gates terminus taking a break from driving and conducting at Eastbourne.** *Seaton Tramway collection.*

and used on the extension, hauling a hopper wagon. The overhead wire used on the new line came from Blackpool.

Once again opportunity was taken to publicise the tramway by an official opening. The Mayor of Eastbourne, Councillor J.W.G. Howlett, opened the line in the traditional way, by driving number 6 from the Depot to the new terminus. The tramcar was filled with distinguished guests, including the Mayoress, Councillors and Borough Officials. They left the Princes Park Gates terminus at 2.15pm and ran along the line to a tape marking where the extension started. The tramcar broke through the tape, officially opening the new section, bringing the line up to its maximum length of approximately 1 mile.

The Mayor drove the tramcar back to the Princes Park Gates where he addressed the assembled crowd, including a reference to the fact that this was the narrowest gauge passenger carrying tramway running double deck trams in the world. He wished it every success in the future. Then he drove the tramcar to the depot where refreshments had been laid on for all the guests. Here the Mayor was presented with a framed photograph of himself on the tram at the beginning of the festivities. Mr Jordan, of the local photographers Harry C. Deal, had taken the photograph, processed it and had it framed in the short time available.

BBC Television sent a crew to film the event, using 225 again as the camera tram, getting shots of Councillor Howlett driving the tram along the new line. The film was broadcast on the following Wednesday. The following two days saw record crowds visiting the line, many coming from considerable distances.

It had always been the intention to continue the tramway to Langney Point. However, this would have meant using land near to the Chatsworth Estates. It was quite clear from experience of the previous extension that such an extension would be opposed. In addition Claude had been told informally that the Corporation were concerned that if the tramway was extended it would harm the takings of their buses on that route. So all ideas of further extensions had to be shelved.

### 1958/9 – The Barnet Factory Closes

1958 was a notable year for another reason. Claude decided that it would be better to be based entirely at Eastbourne, rather than splitting the company between Barnet and Eastbourne. Planning permission was obtained to build a large new workshop and administrative offices for Modern Electric Tramways on the Princes Park site. This was given and work began on the new building, which cost £2,000. The Coseley Engineering Company of Wolverhampton erected the main structural framework, while the timber and brickwork were constructed by local firms. The workshops were connected to the line by a short branch from the depot. The new line had some ex-Hendon gas lights which had fluted standards and ornate scrollwork.

Inside the shops were two tracks, each with maintenance pits. These tracks used grooved tram rail that had originally been made for the Leeds City tramways.

The additional building space also allowed the company to generate its own power supply and become independent of the mains supply. Two Lister Blackstone diesel engines were transferred from the Barnet works to Eastbourne and used to drive the two Crompton dynamos which produced the electrical power for the tramway. The engines had been in use at Barnet for 32 years before the transfer. The larger engine, which developed an output of 10kW, started its life as a show engine. It lit the Blackstone exhibition stand at the 1931 "Royal Show" in Ipswich. As soon as the show ended it was taken to the Lancaster Electrical Company Works. When it arrived at Eastbourne it was given a complete overhaul and repaint. The other engine, built in 1932, was smaller, producing 4.5kW. The two dynamos had a working voltage of 120 volts and this was stepped down to 72 volts for the tramway. They also charged up a standby battery, which was used during less busy periods, allowing the engines and dynamos to be maintained. It was planned to build a new depot alongside the works and remove the old depot building, but other events meant that this was never to be achieved. Above the generator room was a store room, office and wash room. Once a week Claude would devote a day to office administration, a task that he intensely disliked but that he knew had to be done. Staff and volunteers knew it was wise to steer clear of him on the office days.

**The newly built headquarters and workshop building. Note the old gates which were replaced by the wrought iron gates from Hendon Works.** *Photograph Gordon Gangloff.*

**Looking at the new Headquarters building from the depot loop.** *Seaton Tramway collection.*

The new works building also served an additional, less official function, as accommodation for Claude. He had a bed fitted at the far end with an electric heater and, it was reported, surrounded by empty half pint milk bottles.

In addition to the power for the trams the generators also supplied power to the workshops, lighting in the offices and external lights along the tramway route. Two feeder cables that were connected to the overhead wire and rails, at intervals along the track, supplied the power to the tramway.

The year also saw, in May, the appointment of Allan Gardner as a Director of Modern Electric Tramways. Another new tramcar also entered service. Number 7 was the last car to be built in the Barnet

**Car 23 arriving in Glasgow after being sold to the Scottish Tramway Museum Society.** *Seaton Tramway collection.*

**Car 23 in the garden of the STMS Secretary.** *Seaton Tramway collection.*

Works and on completion was taken to Eastbourne. It was built to the same general design as the successful number 6. However, two small, enclosed saloons were built at either end of the lower deck to allow shelter in inclement weather (in 1962 number 6 was modified to match).

1958 saw the sale of number 23, the first tram Claude had built. It had returned from Rhyl in 1957 and its small size meant that it was not able to be regauged from its original 15-inch gauge. After storage in the Barnet factory it was sold to the Scottish Tramway Museum Society and moved to Cambuslang. Thankfully number 23 has survived and its full history is given later in the book. Once the move of headquarters to Eastbourne had been completed the old works at Barnet were sold in 1959.

The Crumbles extension increased the fare stages from two to three, and the single-fare structure for 1959 was:

| | Royal Parade | Golf House | Depot |
|---|---|---|---|
| **Golf House** | 2d | | |
| **Depot** | 4d | 2d | |
| **Crumbles** | 6d | 4d | 2d |

A round journey ticket could be purchased from any stage for 10d. An inspector from Eastbourne Corporation would pay random visits and board the trams to check the tickets. While this helped the tramway keep control of the ticket issuing, it was primarily carried out to allow the Corporation to check the numbers of tickets sold, as their income was a percentage of ticket sales. It is interesting to note that the inspector never once found anyone trying to travel without a ticket. It is believed that the public never think of not paying on a pleasure line, unlike the attitude towards public transport.

Number 238, while unpopular with the crews, was very much the people's favourite. In August the queues were sometimes four deep and very long. John Price paid one of his many visits to the line and one of the drivers commented that while the regular drivers would keep to the authorised stops, Claude Lane himself was always stopping at the depot, the substation and other points of interest along the line.

## More Extension Proposals

In September 1959 the company made application to extend the tramway from the Crumbles to Langney Point. Mr Cannon, the Corporation Transport Manager, who expressed concerns that the "Toy" amusement ride was attempting to provide a public service, opposed this. His major fear was that the trams would compete with the Corporation buses, or worse, at some stage replace the trams with buses. In November the Council decided to defer a decision for twelve months. The response from the tramway was to ask for an extension in the opposite direction going half a mile from Princes Park Gates to the Redoubt, near to the town and pier. They also pointed out that the fares on the trams were higher than the parallel bus service. Again the decision was deferred.

By 1960, Modern Electric Tramways had settled into the new building, having spent the winter giving the tramcars their usual yearly overhaul, repairs and repaint, while the track and overhead were also checked and repaired. The overhead at the Park Gates terminus was altered, with an automatic trolley reverser being fitted. The two new cars, numbers 6 and 7, had proved a great success, but they did have one shortcoming. Very often trams would arrive at the Crumbles terminus with every seat taken. Often no one would want to alight. Unfortunately there was no room on 6 or 7 for standing passengers. So those waiting at the terminus would be left behind. Often several trams would come in this way and intending passengers would give up and go away, so the tramway lost revenue.

## 1960/1 – Open Boat No. 4 and Busmen's Jitters

To overcome the capacity problems experienced in the previous year the next tram to be built was designed to be able to take additional standing passengers. This was number 4, another open "Boat" design, but considerably larger than numbers 225 and 226. It was designed to seat 20 passengers and take a further 30 standing. Building of the tram started in the winter of 1960 and continued throughout most of 1961.

In October 1960 the company applied to the Committee for a revision of the terms of the agreement. It was agreed that payments would be 15% on the first £2,000 of fares taken and 25% thereafter. No payment would be required in respect of fares taken between 1 October and 31 March (or the Wednesday

**Car 4 when new.** *Seaton Tramway collection.*

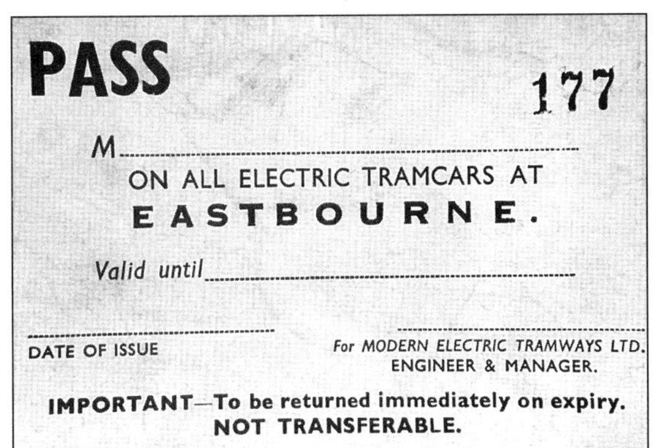

**PASS** 177

M..........................................

ON ALL ELECTRIC TRAMCARS AT

**EASTBOURNE.**

*Valid until*..........................................

............................ DATE OF ISSUE

............................ *For* MODERN ELECTRIC TRAMWAYS LTD. ENGINEER & MANAGER.

**IMPORTANT—To be returned immediately on expiry. NOT TRANSFERABLE.**

**The pass carried by the ticket inspectors.** *Seaton Tramway collection.*

before Easter, whichever was the earlier). Once again the company applied for an extension of the agreement beyond 31 October 1963, but this was refused. The tramway also asked again for an extension of the tramway to Langney Point.

Mr Cannon, the Corporation Transport Manager, continued to have worries over the tramway. He wrote to the Town Clerk insisting that the words "model" or "miniature" should be included in the company's title and again voicing his concern that the trams might be replaced by buses. In October Mr Cannon opposed both the extension of the line and the extension of the agreement. He believed that the tramway company was trying to become a serious rival to the Corporation buses. He suggested to the Council that any agreement should have restrictions in it, so that the tramway would never cross a public highway; the gauge would never exceed 2 feet; they could only run miniature or model trams; they could not substitute any road passenger vehicle for the tram service; that the tramway would never obstruct the Corporation bus service; and that the words "model" or "miniature" should be included in the company's title.

There was a protection arrangement between the Corporation bus service and Southdown Motor Services, where Southdown was excluded from operating any service entirely within the Borough of Eastbourne. A major concern of the Corporation Transport Manager was that the tramway company would sell its shares to Southdown, who would then be allowed to compete directly with the Corporation buses. All this was long before 1986 and the introduction of bus deregulation.

In December 1960 the tramway had another attempt to get permission for an extension, this time only for an extra 10 yards, but it was again refused. This short extension was required to take the tramway to the edge of the Council property. Beyond this point the land belonged to the Chatsworth Estate and Claude felt he could now get agreement from the Estate to continue the tramway to Langney Point. The Council were quite aware of the reason for the request and continued to turn down every application to ensure that the tramway could not be extended.

In 1961 Number 6 was five years old and an indication of the amount of work these small tramcars were asked to do was the 55,000 miles it had travelled carrying passengers – not bad considering that the tramway was mainly a summer season operation. The new Boat tramcar, number 4, was completed and entered service on 23 November 1961, easing the workload of numbers 6 and 7. The tramway was operating daily from 10am to 10pm seven days a week during the season. At either end of the season it operated weekends only and between Christmas and Easter a short Sunday service was provided. At this time the operating voltage was raised to 120 volts to give much needed extra power to the larger trams. The original 60-volt motors were retained but, to enable operation on the higher voltage, the controllers were adjusted so that the motors remained in series and could not be switched to parallel.

In December 1961 half a mile of overhead, worth £40, was stolen one night. The company proposed to the Committee that they could set up a system of lighting along Wartling Road using the traction supply power. The Chief Constable supported the proposal and the Committee agreed, contributing £20 towards the costs.

The fares were collected by conductors on the tramcars and tickets issued using T.I.M. ticket machines. Eastbourne Corporation Inspectors continued to check the conductors and passengers. They could board the trams at any point and inspect all the tickets.

## Problems and Solutions

Operation of the Eastbourne line was not always without incident. One winter they found that the East Sussex River Board had been repairing the sea defences with no regard to the tramway at all. They drove heavy lorries over the track and managed to knock down several traction poles and removed lengths of overhead wire. There was also a constant irritation caused by a combination of children, a pebble beach and boredom. To amuse themselves children would throw pebbles at the overhead traction poles in order to hear the noise it made. Claude would frequently chase them off. One day he was so fed up with it that he gave the culprit a can of paint and a brush and told him to paint the pole, much to the annoyance of the youth.

One evening Claude and Allan were driving trams and had parked both their tramcars at the Crumbles terminus. It had been the day of the annual carnival and they saw one of the floats, on the back of a large lorry, drive past. Claude wondered where the lorry was going and Allan commented that he hoped it was not intending to park in the Golf House car park, because it was too high for the overhead. A moment later they saw the overhead line jerk and the power was cut off. So they walked back towards the depot and sure enough the lorry driver was untangling overhead wire from the display on his lorry. Following this accident longer traction poles were planted where the line crossed the road in order to raise the height of the wire.

**The replica 'B' type bus and car 338 by the depot fan.** *Photograph Gordon Gangloff.*

On another occasion number 4 derailed while it was going across the roadway. Some pebbles had rolled into the rail groove, lifting the wheel and derailing the tramcar. Allan went back to the depot to collect the Morris van, with all the tools and jacks. When he got back Claude and the tramcar were surrounded by a crowd of onlookers. One of them, a bus driver, was very loud in his advice on what to do. Claude was standing quietly, obviously irritated by this "expert". Then the bus driver said that he could not see what the fuss was about, the tram was so small he could lift it back onto the track, probably one handed. This was just the opportunity Claude wanted. He then invited the bus driver to do just that, lift the tram back onto the rails. Claude knew that the tramcar weighed several hundredweight. The bus driver confidently strode forward and grasped the tramcar. Red faced he lifted with all his might, only to find that the tram did not even quiver. After several tries he had to admit defeat. Claude then suggested that he should let the experienced staff do the job.

**The small replica of a 'B' type London bus running along the sea front.** *Photograph Gordon Gangloff.*

**The 'B' type replica near the workshops.** *Seaton Tramway collection.*

## A Diminutive "General"

Trams were not the only vehicles built by Claude Lane. He constructed a replica small London 'B' type bus, built on the chassis of a 1929 Swift car. This was used for publicity purposes. When it was taken to Eastbourne, Claude decided to drive it all the way from Barnet. Through London he was subjected to a constant flow of jokes from the drivers of the real London buses. Claude would pull alongside a bus and watch the driver's expression when he saw the small vintage bus, then would come the jokes.

At Eastbourne Claude would use the bus on any opportunity, as publicity. One evening he needed to pop down to the local shops, so he took the bus. Parking it outside the shop he went inside and found himself waiting behind an old man. When he had been served the old man walked out of the shop, only to rush back in saying that there was an old bus outside and not just any old bus, but the actual one he drove in London. Claude went out with him and allowed him to look inside the bus. The old driver got rather puzzled, saying he did not remember the stairs being so small. Claude reassured him by saying that people were much smaller in those days!

**Car 3 tucked at the back of the workshops with car 2 almost complete and ready for service.** ***Seaton Tramway collection.***

## 1962 – The Small Trams become Redundant

Number 3 was very popular. However, this popularity was proving to be a big disadvantage. Nearly all the passengers wanted to ride on its top deck. This caused a major problem. Being the smallest tramcar access to the upper deck was awkward. So, despite having the fewest passengers, it took longer than any of the other trams for its passengers to board and alight. To compound the problem people would miss a ride on one of the other cars in order to wait for number 3. Again many potential customers were put off by large queues at the terminus. So number 3, together with numbers 225 and 238, was not modified for the higher 120 volts and so could not be used. Claude decided that another large tram was needed.

In October 1962 the tramway managed to get some more publicity for their proposals to extend the system. The London Evening Standard published an article on the extension proposals. It detailed that extensions were being sought to reach west to the Redoubt and east to Langney Point. This would double the length of the line to nearly two miles. In the same article it was stated that 175,000 passengers had been carried by the tramway in 1961 and more than 100,000 in the summer of 1962.

The same month the Town Clerk prepared a report on the tramway for the Council. He stated that the yearly receipts for the operation from 1958 were between £1,800 and £2,000. In his view the operation was run on a shoe-string. He then referred to the request for a westward extension to take the tramway nearer to the town centre and to the 10-yard extension to the Chatsworth Estate boundary. He stated that Mr Lane had expressed hopes that the tramway would run to Pevensey Bay, which would seriously affect the

**Car 238 loaded on a lorry ready for the start of its journey to America.** *Seaton Tramway collection.*

**Cars 3 and 225 loaded for the journey to the ship.** *Seaton Tramway collection.*

Corporation bus operation. His conclusions were that the Council should not allow any westward extension. They could allow extensions in the other direction, but should only do so with restrictions that would ensure that the tramway would not compete against the buses.

## 1963 – Three Tramcars go to America

The year saw an unexpected reduction in the number of tramcars. Mr Don Sorenson, a garage owner from Wilton, Connecticut, had heard about the tramway and spent a week in Eastbourne. He rode on the tramway and was entirely captivated by the small trams. He walked around the depot and saw the three smallest trams, numbers 3, 225 and 238. When he asked about them he was told that they were out of use. He decided to purchase them and negotiated with Claude. At this time Claude was thinking about building a new tramcar and the money raised by the sale of the small trams would go a long way to paying for the new car. Mr Sorenson then spent two weeks working at the Eastbourne Tramway learning tramcar maintenance and repair.

The tramcars left Eastbourne on 25 November 1963 to be taken by road to the Royal Victoria Docks in the Port of London. Here they were loaded onto the *SS American Champion* which sailed to New York, arriving on 8 December. Claude had pasted a notice on Number 3 saying "GREETINGS FROM THE TRAMWAY AT EASTBOURNE, ENGLAND TO WILTON CONN. USA". The American press took up the story and there was considerable publicity, all of which quoted the greetings notice. The trams were then taken by road, on a boat trailer, from New York to Mr Sorenson's home in Wilton, Connecticut. He had three children, Roy, Donna and Keith, then respec-

**Car 3 being loaded into the hold of the ship bound for America.** *Seaton Tramway collection.*

**Car 3 in the garden in Wilton, Connecticut.** *Seaton Tramway collection.*

**All three trams in Don Sorenson's garden in America.** *Seaton Tramway collection.*

tively 12, 9 and 4 years old, and he gave each of them a tram of their own. He laid 520 feet of track and 200 feet of sidings in his back garden. He did not erect overhead wire, choosing instead to install five 12-volt batteries in each car to give the required 60 volts. The trams were an immediate hit with the local children, though the gong pedals on the trams had to be removed in order that the adults could keep their sanity.

Back in Eastbourne, September saw a rare accident on the line. On a Sunday evening car 6 overturned as it was taking the curve just past the depot on the way to the Crumbles. Luckily there were only four passengers aboard. The tram was moving at a normal speed and it appeared that the rear bogie had split the points leading to a short stub siding. This made the car slew and it fell on to its side. No one was hurt and number 4 operated a short service between Park Gates and the Depot.

The agreement with the

**Car 2 at Langney Point terminus.** *Photograph John Meredith.*

Entertainments and Pleasure Grounds Committee was to terminate on 31 October 1963. It was not until 20 September that the Committee agreed to a one year extension to 31 October 1964. In 1964 the return fare was raised from 10 pence to 1 shilling, the reason given was that the tramway was making very little profit. Claude asked the Council if they would agree not to take their percentage from the 2 pence increase. The Council refused.

## 1964 – Enter Number 2

The new tramcar that Claude had started to build in 1963 was now introduced This was number 2, which was designed using many features from the Metropolitan Electric Tramways Company "A" Type tramcars. These had open tops and a form of straight staircase with a half landing called "Robinson" stairs (named after the general manager of the London United Tramways Company who used the design on the LUT tramcars). Number 2 had a lower deck in a

**Car 2 going into service from the workshops, the driver is changing the points for it to pass onto the main track.** *Photograph R. B. Parr.*

**The Metropolitan Electric Tramways gates from Hendon workshops.** *Seaton Tramway collection.*

similar style to numbers 6 and 7. The ends of number 2 were different to 6 and 7 because the upper deck extends only to the bulkhead – in tramway parlance this design is described as "uncanopied".

## Second-Hand Depot Gates

In October 1964 Claude and Allan were motoring up to Macclesfield and drove through London. Whenever he was in North London Claude would always drive past the old Hendon Tramway workshops, as a reminder of his childhood days spent outside the works waiting for trams to come out. However, on this occasion he got a shock. The building had been razed to the ground and the boundary wall was also demolished. However the external gates and pillars were still standing, alone among the building site. Claude was saddened by the sight and wondered what would happen to the gates. Allan suggested writing to London Transport to ask if he could purchase them, after all it would only cost a stamp. Claude did write and to their surprise received a reply saying that if he could arrange transport he could have them. So as soon as possible he and Allan took the lorry to London and arrived at the site. They showed the site manager the letter and he readily agreed, helping with the loading of the gates on to the lorry. Then he asked did they know there was another pair of gates? Claude said that they were the gates for the workshop area. The site manager then told him that they were on the ground around the back and they could take those as well. Claude needed no further encouragement and so they drove back to Eastbourne with two pairs of Hendon gates.

After unloading the gates Claude raised one, leaning it against the wall to get an idea of what they would look like when erected. They stood back and admired it. When Claude went to walk past it, it became unbalanced and fell on top of him, pinning him to the ground. Quickly the staff lifted the gate off him, to find that he had gashed his face badly. So it meant a trip to the local hospital accident department. Here he had to try to explain that a tram depot gate falling on him had caused his injury.

The Corporation Transport Department were still pre-occupied with the notion that the Tramway posed a potential threat to their bus services. With this in mind Claude undertook a charm offensive on Mr Cannon, part of which included inviting him to tour the works. Mr Cannon was suspicious of these overtures, but he did visit the workshop. What he saw horrified him. This was a new, totally enclosed single deck tram. At 31ft 6in. long and 4ft 10in. wide it was considerably bigger than the other trams. Designed for 2ft 9in. gauge operation it was initially mounted on the Eastbourne 2ft gauge bogies. This new 40-seater was no "toy" tram and it confirmed his fears that the tramway was trying to take over the bus service.

This new tram took two years to complete, entering service as number 12 in 1966. It was designed to be suitable for winter operation as well as during wet or cold weather in the summer season. Although the local

**Car 12 by the Yacht club. This was originally called the Artisan's Sailing Club, by the time 12 was constructed it had become the Sovereign Sailing Club.** *Photograph Brian Wainwright.*

**The Tram Shop, 01, at Park Gates terminus.** *Photograph Geoff Tribe.*

council proclaimed Eastbourne as the "Sun Trap of the South", Claude often referred to it as the *wind*-trap of the South.

## A Mobile Solution to Theft

During the 1964 season the small kiosk at Princes Park terminus that sold tickets for the trams and a small range of gifts suffered a series of break-ins. Something had to be done and Claude's solution was to have a sales kiosk that could be locked away during the night. So the unique electric tram-shop was built in 1964/5. The flat bed works car 01 was taken into the workshop and rebuilt into the Tram Shop. It began its new role at the start of the 1965 season. In this way it became one of the most famous of all the trams at Eastbourne, continuing in the same role for many more years at Seaton. Like the kiosk it enabled waiting passengers to buy their tickets in advance, effectively locking them into riding on the tramway. Advantage was also taken to sell souvenirs, postcards, books and other gifts. To accommodate the shop an extra stub-end was laid at Princes Park terminus.

The days now started with the Tram Shop being driven out to the terminus, showing everyone that the tramway was open. It was usually Claude who drove the shop out to the terminus. The Tram Shop was one of only two known in the world. The only other similar vehicle was to be found at Douglas on the Isle of Man, where the horse tramway has a Tram Shop that is parked outside the depot. However, the Douglas shop sells just souvenirs, fares being paid on the horse trams.

**The shop on a busy day with plenty of customers.** *Seaton Tramway collection.*

## 1965/6 – The End is Nigh

In September 1964 the Entertainments and Pleasure Grounds Committee had given a further one year extension to the tramway, so it could now operate to 31 October 1965. This yearly extension of the agreement was most unsatisfactory for Claude, so in September 1965 he approached the Committee requesting a seven-year extension for the tramway. He explained that it was very difficult to make improvements when arrangements were on a year-to-year basis. In the last twelve months 150 yards of track had been renewed at a cost of £300. Since most of the track had been on site for eleven years and some had been used for three years previously to that, the company wished to renew it. However, before doing so the company would want security of tenure. However the Town Clerk reminded the Committee that it was shortly necessary for the Council to carry out the second review of the Development Plan and that the future development of the Crumbles area would have to be included. The

**The stretch of track from the depot to Golf House was doubled to allow a more frequent service.** *Seaton Tramway collection.*

Borough Surveyor referred to the likely construction of new highways in the vicinity of the tramway. This came as a shock to Claude and the company.

The immediate reaction of Claude was to appeal against the decision. But he found that he was constantly being put off. The decision was delayed and delayed. The Council first suggested that the whole line could be moved southwards to allow room for the road. Claude countered by suggesting that they could support the extensions to Langney Point one way and The Redoubt the other. Time continued to pass and Claude began to have thoughts that it was a repeat of the St Leonard's experience.

At the next meeting, in October, Claude appeared before the Committee accompanied by his Solicitor Mr Brewer. They were asked if the tramway company was going to sell its rights to an omnibus company. Claude gave a categorical assurance that no approaches had been made and the company had no intention of disposing of their undertaking to any other company. The Committee were worried that a commercial bus company might get the tramway and then claim passenger service rights in Eastbourne. At the same meeting the Committee agreed by four votes to three to give a further period of three years on the agreement, so it now expired on 31 October 1968. However, the extension was subject to resiting the track in accordance with the instructions of the Borough Surveyor and additionally the possible resiting of the tramway works building. Claude and Mr Brewer were back in front of the Committee on 16 February 1966, this time to tell them that the terms of 15 October 1965 were unacceptable to the company. Therefore the agreement had run out on 31 October 1965 and the tramway had no legal rights to operate or keep their buildings and equipment.

In regard to the tramway, the solicitor put a counter offer including the Langney Point extension, removal of the condition to resite the main workshop at six months notice and for the agreement to be longer than three years. After Claude and his solicitor had withdrawn the Town Clerk strongly recommended the Committee to adhere to their October 1965 decision. This was approved. The company had to rethink their position. Up to that point Claude felt he had a chance to get a reasonable agreement. But when he discovered that the Town Clerk was no longer supporting the tramway and was advising the Council to cease the concession Claude realised that his days at Eastbourne were numbered. So he started seriously looking for another site. They went back to the Committee in March prepared to enter into an agreement provided that notice to move the main workshop was not served during the period 1 December to 30 March, so they would not have to resite the building during the summer and subject to the company having the right to terminate the agreement on the expiry of the notice, instead of carrying out the resiting required.

**Track maintenance at Park Gates.** *Seaton Tramway collection.*

**Car 12 at Langney Point with Claude Lane turning the trolley pole.** *Photograph Howard Butler.*

This was agreed by three votes to one. The tramway was able to continue to operate for a while longer.

## Another Search for a New Home

With all his previous experiences Claude was now determined that any new site would have to be a free-hold purchase to allow him to have complete control of the future of the tramway and no longer be subject to the quirks of a landlord. This was the time of the Beeching railway plans and many small branch lines were being closed.

Through a friend of his former nanny, Claude found that the Bridport to West Bay branch in Dorset was closing. Claude visited the line and it looked as if it had potential for the trams. So he got in contact with British Railway Estates and was passed to an aptly named Mr Lines. They met at the line to talk over the possibilities of a purchase. Things looked good, but British Railways were required to give the offer of purchase to the local council first. It turned out that the Council said that they had plans to lay a new outfall pipeline across the railway line. Claude decided to visit the planning department because he thought he might get agreement to have the line after the outfall was laid. During the visit the Planning officer told Claude that the Council now intended to build a new road that needed some of the railway, effectively rendering the line worthless for the tramway.

As they left the meeting the Planning Officer said to Claude that if he did not have to go back that night he could visit the Seaton Branch the next day, as that too was due to close. This Claude decided to do, and after staying overnight he drove to Seaton. As he approached from Lyme Regis he saw the great beauty of the East Devon countryside. He talked to some of the local people and they seemed enthusiastic, so he decided to contact Mr Lines again about purchasing the Seaton branch. Thankfully Claude did not realise he was entering a five and half year project just to purchase the line.

Back in Eastbourne, in October the Entertainments and Pleasure Grounds Committee sat again and the Borough Surveyor gave more details of the new road. Effectively the majority of the tramway would need to be relocated. Only the section from the depot to the Crumbles would not be affected. The depot building itself would need to be moved. The Committee authorised the Town Clerk to serve notice on the tramway company to resite the track by 31 October 1967.

At a meeting on 10 February 1967 it was reported that the road building would be deferred for a year, so the tramway might be able to be given an extension to 31 October 1968. In October 1967 the Committee confirmed that the tracks could stay until October 1968. The new road depended upon Sussex River Authority to reconstruct the Crumbles outfall. The timetable was for the outfall work to be completed by October 1967 and the road was to be built in 1968. In the event the River authority did not complete the culvert until 1968, so the Council put the scheme back a year. So the final date for the removal of the tramway was set as 31 October 1969 and the company aimed for September as the last running month.

## A Very Unofficial Extension!

One morning Claude was late getting to the tramway. So when he reached the depot he was in a hurry to take the shop out. He was driving beside the Wartling Road when the trolley pole came off the wire. Claude found that the electric brake would not work. Unfortunately, as the tram shop was only driven a short distance each day, the hand brake was not as efficient as on the other trams. So the shop carried on, unchecked, to the end of the line and then a bit further.

Allan got a phone call from Claude to take the van and tools to the terminus. Here he found the shop well clear of the end of the rails, having been brought to a halt by the fence. Allan looked at the distance back to the track and asked Claude if he was trying to drive to France! Claude was far from amused and the rescue operation was carried out in stony silence. To Allan's relief he had to go back to the depot to fetch a length of temporary track. They had to haul 01 back on to the rails via the temporary track and then to the terminus.

**The huts behind the tram were used by the contractors building the new road. This is the last year of the operation of the tramway.** *Seaton Tramway collection.*

The first passengers of the day were given a free demonstration on re-railing a tramcar.

## 1967 – Devon Beckons

Thoughts were now very much on the new line at Seaton. This was going to be much longer than at Eastbourne and offered all kinds of opportunities. The first was the chance to achieve what had been planned since the building of number 6, to increase the track gauge again – this time to 2ft 9in. So plans were put in place to build a new tramcar, number 8.

This was to be the last tram to be completed at Eastbourne. Using the same basic design as numbers 6 and 7 this tramcar pushed the size of the trams a little more. It was three feet longer and 4 inches wider. The trucks were also to the wider gauge of 2 feet 9 inches, ready for use on the Seaton line. Completion was in 1968.

**In this photograph the trams are on the double track between the Golf House and the depot, the line to the workshop goes across the centre, while the line to Langney Point can be seen along the horizon.** *Photograph Geoff Tribe.*

## 1968 – A New Works Car

By now there were five operational passenger trams (numbers 2, 4, 6, 7, and 12), with number 8 in readiness for the next move. There were two works cars (numbers 01 and 02).

Works car 02, which had been the Air Ministry order, was a four wheel vehicle. However, there would be virtually no road access to the Seaton line, and the tramway would need a railborne works car that would be able to carry all the material, operate on battery power, allow work on the line and be a shelter in inclement weather. So Claude decided to rebuild number 02.

**Another view of the double track section with spoil heaps from the construction of the new road on the left.** *Photograph Roger Monk.*

First it was cut in half and a new section put in the middle to lengthen it and increase the capacity of the wagon. The four wheel truck was removed and replaced by bogies. A tower for overhead working was added to the middle of the tram. The interior was fitted with a work bench, vice, drilling machine and equipment. It was also fitted with batteries to allow it to run before the overhead was fitted. It was completed in readiness for the move to Seaton.

## 1969 – Goodbye to Eastbourne

This saw the last year of operation at Eastbourne, but for Modern Electric Tramways the big pressure was to obtain the necessary approval for the building of the Seaton line, which is described in more detail in the next chapter. Back at Eastbourne the tramcars were fitted with special notices saying "LAST TRAM WEEKS This year we say goodbye to Eastbourne. We hope to be running at Seaton Devon next season. Come and enjoy 3 miles of beautiful scenery." These were very reminiscent to the notices carried by London trams in their last week which said "LAST TRAM WEEK This week we say goodbye to London".

## M.E.T. 94 is Slimmed Down to No. 14

While thoughts were on the major move to Seaton, activities still went on in the workshop and a start was made on another tramcar. The history of this tramcar went back to 1960 when a group of tramway enthusiasts discovered the body of Metropolitan Electric Tramways number 94 (later London Transport 2455) in an orchard in Upshire, near Waltham Cross. In 1961 the upper deck was removed and by agreement with Claude Lane the lower deck was moved to its new home, the side of the Eastbourne workshops. The plan was that the group would rebuild the tramcar to its open-top condition as built in 1904. However, work progressed very slowly. The group was having to learn new skills and techniques as well as actually repair the tram. So a new view was taken in 1968 and the body was given to Modern Electric Tramways for them to convert the parts into a new narrow gauge single deck tramcar to run at Seaton. The lower saloon was left the same length, but the platforms were shortened, since there was no need to make room for a staircase. The width of the tramcar was reduced by cutting a section out of the middle of the saloon for the full length of the car. By the time of the move to Seaton the tramcar was a basic wooden frame.

The Entertainments and Pleasure Grounds Committee were still unsure what the timetable for the new road would be. The delays in

**The company lorry, a converted bus which was second-hand when it was used to take the trams to Rhyl, then to Eastbourne and then did numerous trips to Seaton.** *Photograph D. N. Warren.*

**The other company transport was another second-hand bus. This was also used to take the tramway to Seaton.** *Photograph D. N. Warren.*

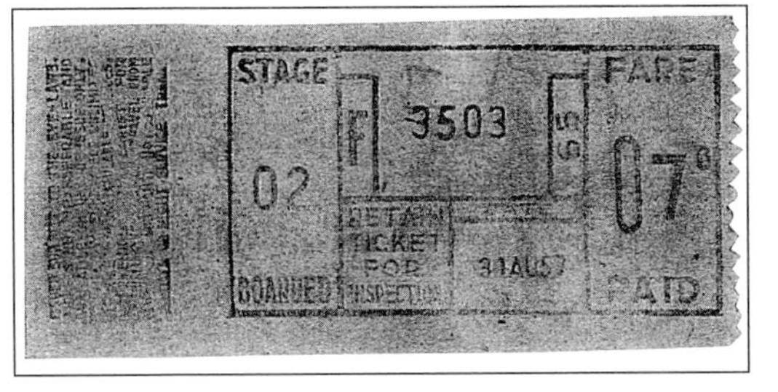


**A few second-hand Ticket Issuing Machines were purchased and used on the tramway. The previous owner crossed out their name and conditions printed at the end of the ticket.** *Courtesy David Padgham.*

**The disruption caused by the new road is clearly seen here. Temporary rails had to be laid across the road to allow trams to get from the workshops to the running line.** *Photograph M. G. Collignon.*

completing the culvert had set back the start of the new road by many months. So at their meeting on 16 May 1969 the Town Clerk reported that the company was prepared to remove the necessary track within 21 days provided the Council would either agree to an alternative use for the Workshop or pay reasonable compensation. They then considered an application by Messrs Lambourne and Bradford for permission to use the Workshop as a children's pleasure centre, with amusement machines and children's rides. The Committee turned down the application and added that no land would be made available for the erection of a building for that use. At the 30 June meeting the Town Clerk reported that the tramway had indicated they would cease operations at Eastbourne. The company had agreed to a compensation sum of £500 plus a sum to be negotiated for the loss of income between the date of ceasing operation and the end of the season. There were four offers for the workshop from boat firms and a sum of £3,000 was being discussed. But the Council refused to give permission to reuse the building and it looked as if the company would have to demolish it.

**A view of the new road alongside the tramway, but it cuts across the line behind the camera.** *Photograph M. G. Collignon.*

**Another view of the precarious temporary track laid over the road.** *Photograph M. G. Collignon.*

**The Metropolitan Electric Tramways body stored in the workshop.** *Seaton Tramway collection.*

A great deal of time and effort of the company was going into getting the necessary Transfer Order and Light Railway Order for Seaton. Indeed the Transfer Order was not granted until Christmas Eve 1969. But this was not an occasion to celebrate and relax. It was the beginning of the task to build the Seaton tramway and the planning for the move of all the equipment from Eastbourne, a 150-mile journey. When the last tram ran in Eastbourne on 14 September 1969 it was the signal for dismantling the whole system, ready for the move.

**A rare view inside the workshops.** *Photograph M. G. Collignon.*

**What car 14 looked like before it was rebuilt into the magnificent tramcar it is today.** *Photograph M. G. Collignon.*

# CHAPTER 5

# The Seaton Line and Building the Tramway

The Seaton Tramway is laid on the track bed of the British Rail Seaton Branch. The origins of this branch go back to 1863 when Parliament passed the Seaton and Beer Railway Act. This Act authorised the building of a single railway line to link with the London and South Western Railway (LSWR) main line at Seaton Junction (between Honiton and Axminster). The line ran from the junction across countryside to Colyton Town, where there were two sidings and then on to Colyford, a small halt platform on the single line. From here the railway ran down the Axe Valley, alongside the river, to the terminus at Seaton, a short distance from the sea front.

Progress on building the railway was very slow owing to problems first with contractors and then with the company running out of money. The line finally opened on 15th March 1868. Although owned by the Seaton and Beer Railway Company (SBR) the railway was operated under contract by the LSWR. There was always antagonism between the two companies, with the SBR always feeling that they were being short changed by the LSWR.

Finally in 1879 the SBR approached the GWR and LSWR to see if either would purchase the branch and if so what price they would pay. Since the line linked with the LWSR it was very unlikely that the GWR was interested and the LSWR dragged their heels. But eventually a contract was finalised and on 3rd January 1888 the line was passed over to the LSWR. As part of a major railway operator the branch prospered. It was a popular holiday line, taking families to Seaton and particularly in later years to the Warner's Holiday Camp that was close to the station. However the 1960s saw the national railway review by Beeching and in order to reduce the costs of British Railways many branch lines were closed. Despite the strong holiday trade the Seaton branch was among those selected and the branch closed on 7th March 1966.

When Claude Lane first visited the line, while he was searching for a suitable site for his tramway in 1964, the railway was still in operation. Like most visitors to Seaton he approached the town on the B3172. For the last couple of miles the road runs on the other side of the river from the railway. The evening was clear and the sun was beginning to set. Claude was able to look across the river, with all its wild life, to the railway. At the same time a two carriage diesel unit trundled down to the terminus. The scene was idyllic and Claude realised that this would be ideal for his tramway. On reaching Seaton he had a chat to some of the townsfolk and found them receptive to the idea of having a tramway to replace the railway when it closed.

Claude contacted British Railway Estates and began negotiations for the purchase of the land. Nothing further happened until the line closed in 1966. Only then were British Railway Estates in a position to start the sales. The local council had first option on the land and they indicated that they would purchase Seaton Station for conversion to industrial units. Modern Electric Tramways then took an option on track bed from the station approach up to and including Colyton Station, roughly three miles long. The track bed north of Colyton was purchased by farmers to extend their fields.

### Purchasing the Old Railway

Without the station area it was necessary for Modern Electric Tramways to ensure they had a terminus within easy access and if possible within sight of the road. Taking a close look at the possibilities Claude felt that the best place for the terminus of the tramway would be closer to the town centre, alongside the public car park. It would be possible to reach the car park by laying track along the northern and western edges of the holiday camp. This would allow the northern approaches to the station to be used as the tram depot and offices. An access road was provided across the station site to the proposed tramway depot.

The land was not purchased immediately because without the necessary authority to build the tramway the land would be of no use to the company. So the negotiations were carried out on the basis that the sale would only go ahead after authorisation had been obtained. The price was £7,500. Claude began his negotiations with the local and county councils. Apart from some lengthy discussions about the road crossing at Colyford, both the Seaton Urban District Council and Devon County Council felt that the tramway would be both a useful local transport and a tourist attraction. They gave their support to the scheme, though to get full support the tramway agreed that the level crossing at Colyford would be protected by standard level crossing flashing lights and that no overhead wires would be fitted. The council felt that the height of the overhead wire at 16 feet 10 inches was unsafe. So it was agreed that trams would travel across the road using battery power.

British Rail obtained the Seaton and Beer Light Railway Order on 18th June 1969. It was then necessary to get a Transfer Order to pass the Light Railway Order to Modern Electric Tramways. The application

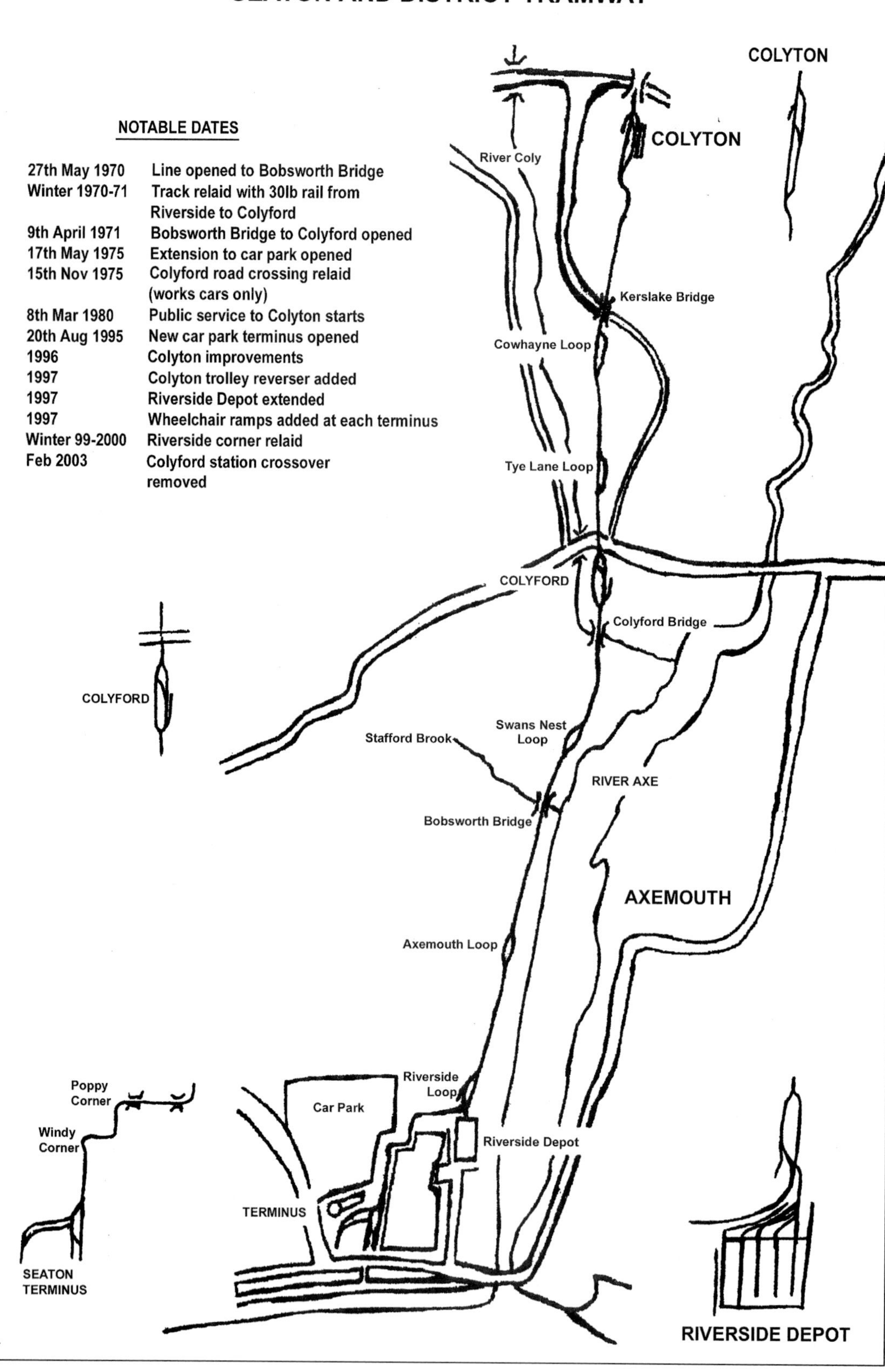
SEATON AND DISTRICT TRAMWAY
NOTABLE DATES
27th May 1970 Line opened to Bobsworth Bridge
Winter 1970-71 Track relaid with 30lb rail from Riverside to Colyford
9th April 1971 Bobsworth Bridge to Colyford opened
17th May 1975 Extension to car park opened
15th Nov 1975 Colyford road crossing relaid (works cars only)
8th Mar 1980 Public service to Colyton starts
20th Aug 1995 New car park terminus opened
1996 Colyton improvements
1997 Colyton trolley reverser added
1997 Riverside Depot extended
1997 Wheelchair ramps added at each terminus
Winter 99-2000 Riverside corner relaid
Feb 2003 Colyford station crossover removed
COLYTON
COLYTON
River Coly
Kerslake Bridge
Cowhayne Loop
Tye Lane Loop
COLYFORD
Colyford Bridge
COLYFORD
Swans Nest Loop
Stafford Brook
RIVER AXE
Bobsworth Bridge
AXEMOUTH
Axemouth Loop
Riverside Loop
Car Park
Riverside Depot
TERMINUS
Poppy Corner
Windy Corner
SEATON TERMINUS
RIVERSIDE DEPOT

**The first stage was the construction of the depot building. Here the building is complete and the first load of rail has been brought from Eastbourne.** *Seaton Tramway collection.*

was publicised and anyone with objections could put their views forward. 600 objections were made. These were addressed and the number reduced to 90. This meant that there had to be a public enquiry. The enquiry was set up on 19th November 1969 and conducted by Mr K.A.S. Philips. The objections ranged from concern that the tramway would spoil the natural beauty of the Axe Valley, to farmers who felt that the trams would scare their cows. Another local resident felt that passengers sitting on the upper deck of the trams would be able to see into their bedroom windows. Another complained that if the tramway failed the local people would be left with rusting pylons and abandoned, multi-coloured tram bodies. Some were reassured during the hearing and withdrew their objections. The inquiry also heard the support from the councils and also the Seaton Chamber of Trade who felt that as a tourist attraction the line would bring welcome trade to the area.

**The back of the depot at Riverside, Seaton. Note the dual gauge track for unloading tramcars brought from Eastbourne and the caravan for overnight stops.** *Seaton Tramway collection.*

## Moving to Seaton

Claude was told on Christmas Eve that the inquiry had decided to allow the application and so the Seaton and Beer Transfer Order 1970 was passed. In anticipation of this Messrs Tyler of Tonbridge were commissioned to import a prefabricated building from Belgium, 105 feet long and 45 feet wide and erect it on the Seaton site for a total price of £10,000. The building was to serve as a four road tram depot, generating station, workshop and headquarters offices. It was erected early in 1970 so the transfer of material from Eastbourne could be started. February 1970 saw the first of 32 round trips, each 344 miles long, by the two company lorries, a Leyland PS1 (which had once been a Yorkshire Traction coach) and a Bedford 11 ton truck and a 6 wheel trailer made by Allan. Most of the 32 return journeys were made by Claude and Allan at night. They moved the whole of the workshop and machinery, nine tramcars, track and points, 160 traction poles, overhead wire and equipment, generators and dynamos, batteries and the many tons of stores. One night Allan was rather lucky – he found the brakes on the lorry acting strangely as he drove through Lyme Regis, but thought little of it. On arriving at Seaton he parked the lorry and headed for bed. In the morning he found a pool of brake fluid under the lorry. A brake pipe had broken and was leaking rapidly. With the steep hills in the locality he felt rather lucky to have got back safely.

Three temporary two foot gauge tracks were laid in the depot for the trams to be initially stored. One of the tracks was laid dual gauge with a third rail set at 2 feet 9 inches gauge. The 2 feet 9 inches gauge had been chosen so that ex British Railway sleepers could be purchased and when cut in half lengthways gave two sleepers suitable for the new tramway. This gave a considerable saving compared to any larger gauge. Among the items transferred were the four ex-MET gates saved from Hendon.

**The first track is laid, using car 02 on battery power and flat bed wagons to carry rail and sleepers.** *Seaton Tramway collection.*

**Tramway rails are laid on the old railway track bed. Overhead construction will come much later.** *Seaton Tramway collection.*

## Battery Operation

The tramway is a commercial operation so it was necessary to start a passenger service as quickly as possible in order to obtain some income. So the company worked flat out to lay track. The initial terminus was by the depot and a 2 feet 9 inch gauge single track was laid parallel to the river. 30 lb per yard newly rolled flat bottom rail was spiked to ex-British Railways sleepers. Around a mile of track was laid to a small bridge over Stafford Brook. Tram number 8 was re-gauged to two feet nine inches and a battery-carrying four wheel trailer was made. Following a visit by Lt Col Townsend Rose of the Railway Inspectorate on 27th May 1970, it was passed as suitable for public operation. However, the formal transfer did not come until a letter arrived in August 1970 from the Ministry of Transport saying that the final transfer had taken place. So the first passenger carrying tram journey was made at 2.30pm on 28th August by number 8, towing a battery trailer. The tramway operated every day for the remainder of the main summer season. The fare charged was one shilling return (5p) and the bridge soon became known as "Bobsworth Bridge". After the main season the tramway reverted to a Sunday only operation, to allow time to continue developing the line. The Sunday service used car number 12 and ran through to the end of November. November was also a key date because the final tramcar (the body of number 14) was moved from Eastbourne on 25th November arriving at Seaton the next day.

**Car 8 took the honour of being the first tramcar to carry passengers at Seaton.** *Seaton Tramway collection.*

The other tram that was used during this period was 01, the tram shop. It was kept in the depot overnight and then wheeled out each day on the temporary 2 feet gauge track. Here it carried on with its essential role of selling tickets and souvenirs. Claude was eager to see what the system would look like with proper overhead and so was very keen to get a few traction poles erected. Wanting to get started he suggested to Allan that they take a pole out on the back of the lorry. His idea was to dig the hole for the pole, slide it off the back of the lorry into the hole and back the lorry up until the pole was vertical. This sounded very Heath Robinson and potentially dangerous to Allan, but Claude was a difficult man to keep down when he was excited. So out they went in the lorry, the hole was dug and the pole slid off the back of the lorry. Claude then backed the lorry while Allan tried to keep the pole in posi-

**Public operation with battery powered tramcars.** *Seaton Tramway collection.*

**The two white posts mark the end of the track at Bobsworth Bridge. Note the new rail laid alongside the track in order to replace the original rail which was found to be faulty.** *Photograph Geoff Tribe.*

tion. It became very unstable and long before reaching its proper position it slid across the back of the lorry and fell over, narrowly missing Allan. Claude then realised the real danger and gave up until they had proper equipment.

## A Sad Shock

After November 1970 work was carried out to replace the rotting main timbers of Bobsworth Bridge. Once this was completed early in 1971, track laying to Colyford could be undertaken. It was at this time that Claude Lane was taken seriously ill with a heart attack and after spending three weeks in Axminster Hospital he unexpectedly died on 2nd April 1971. His obituary appeared in "Modern Tramway". This untimely and unexpected event hit the organisation very hard. They had lost a close friend and a major driving force behind the tramway. So in addition to the shock and sadness of the loss, there was a void and everyone felt numb. The whole future of Modern Electric Tramways was thrown in turmoil. Despite the shock the organisation continued to operate, but there was a big question mark over the long-term future. Claude had not married and had no immediate descendents.

**Car 8 with the battery trailer. Note the taut rope holding the trolley down while the loose wire takes power from the battery to the trolley head.** *Seaton Tramway collection.*

It fell to the Lane family to unravel Claude's estate. The Leslie Lane family very much wanted the tramway to succeed and it was decided that nephew Roger should join Allan Gardner as a Director and also to assist his father Leslie to act as executor. The position of the company was very precarious. It had just 400 yards of track, no marketing and hardly any customers. There was very little income to offset the substantial costs of the essential development of the tramway. As Claude died intestate, the executors actually had more freedom to transfer funds from the estate to the tramway. From these humble beginnings the Seaton and District Tramway was born.

Neither Allan nor Roger had any formal training in running a company. So it was necessary to quickly learn the lessons of cash flow forecasting, using hand drafted spreadsheets. Persuasion was a necessary skill in order to secure future bank overdraft facilities. Running the company economically was essential and the disciplines learned at that time have remained throughout the continuing development of the tramway, though these days computers and sophisticated techniques are the order of the day.

Meetings of the Directors discussed the situation. As the tramway had started operation, albeit limited, there was an income and fortunately sufficient traffic was being carried to finance the operation. The Directors shared the faith of Claude in the development of the tramway and they decided to continue the development in the way that Claude had planned. They also confirmed Allan Gardner as Managing Director. By now the undertaking had been named the Seaton and District Tramway Company, the operating company of Modern Electric Tramways. In addition many people who admired the tramway contacted Allan to volunteer their services to help the organisation through these difficult times. Allan was extremely grateful for this practical expression of support. It made him realise that there was enormous interest in the tramway and that they might be able to complete Claude's plans without him.

To add to the problems the new rail was found to be unreliable. The rail was fracturing under use. Negotiations with the supplier led to them admitting partial liability due to faulty manufacture and half the rail was returned. Allan rang George Barber at the Romney Hythe and Dymchurch Railway and told him of their problem. Rail was urgently needed and they could not trust their present supplier. George Barber suggested they contact George Cohen's 600 Group, an international specialist scrap metal merchant, as he thought they had some suitable rail available. When Allan contacted the 600 Group he was told that they had 500 tons of 30 lb per yard rail stacked at their docks. It had been reclaimed from a closed section of Sierra Leone Government Railway. Allan went over to look at the rail and found that it was in an almost new condition. Subsequently they found that it was much tougher than the previous rail. He contacted Roger Lane who spoke with the other Directors and it was agreed to go ahead with the purchase. It took several lorries to deliver the rail. They had no crane so the rail was manhandled off the lorries. This was a dangerous manoeuvre with such heavy material. As the last load was being unloaded a rail fell awkwardly and dropped

**Traction poles for the overhead wait at Riverside.** *Seaton Tramway collection.*

**Cars 2 and 8 wait at Riverside depot, both still running with battery trailers.** *Photograph N Rayfield.*

**Traction poles have been erected but are still waiting for overhead wire. Car 8 waits by the ex railway platelayers hut at Axmouth, that was to become the generator station.** *Seaton Tramway collection.*

**Car 8, as rebuilt, in the depot.** *Photograph Geoff Tribe.*

**Allan Gardner and Richard Lane dig a hole for an overhead traction pole.** *Seaton Tramway collection.*

onto Allan's foot. Luckily he had not broken any bones, but it was a nasty moment and he was badly bruised for some time.

Having got the replacement rail meant that the whole line from the depot to Colyford had to be relaid. All planned development had to be shelved for the year and the overhead erection was equally set back. Every moment was used to lift the inferior track and relay the new rail. At the same time the opportunity was taken to install passing loops. The layout now consisted of a single track from the depot to Colyford, with three passing loops. One by the depot, called Riverside Loop, one before Bobsworth bridge, named Axmouth Loop and the final one north of Bobsworth Bridge called Swan's Nest Loop. The points were designed and built by the workshop, though machining of the blades and frogs was contracted out to a local engineering company.

The battery trailer operation between the depot and Colyford recommenced on 9th April 1971. The confidence of the Directors in Claude's plans was affirmed at the end of the year when it was discovered that the income for the year was higher than at any year in Eastbourne, despite the limitations of the service. In addition the local population were able to make a full assessment of the impact of the line on their lives. They found that the trams were not the noisy, dirty vehicles they had imagined. The moving trams were not an eyesore and they were bringing in extra visitors. Not only that but the staff and volunteers on the tramway were friendly and cheerful.

Locals had many opportunities to inspect the tramway close-up, including the evening specials run from Seaton to Colyford where the Young Conservatives held a regular dance night at the White Hart. Allan would drive the tram and park at Colyford, waiting until the dance was over. During these waits he gained the acquaintance of Sue Chaplyn, who was working in the pub. Sue, daughter of Beryl and Cyril Chaplyn, was born on 11th July 1952 in Bishops Stortford, Hertfordshire, the youngest of four children. Sue moved to Seaton with her parents when she was 11, having had many family holidays in the area. Friendship blossomed and they became engaged in 1972. It was inevitable that she would be drawn into the tramway and she became Company Secretary in April 1973. Sue and Allan were married in September 1973 in Axminster Church.

## Volunteer Help

By 1973 there were four employees including Allan's father in law, Cyril Chaplyn and his son David. On many weekends there were working parties of volunteers and enthusiasts who came from all over the country to help the tramway. During the difficult times the Chaplyn family provided tremendous support with accommodation and wonderful Sunday lunches for huge numbers. Without this volunteer help the development of the tramway would have, at best, been delayed by many years. In addition to the invaluable physical effort the volunteers also provided psychological support. Their enthusiasm and faith in the tramway was a tremendous vote of confidence in the decision of the family to see the

**Riverside loop by the depot.** *Seaton Tramway collection.*

**Bobsworth bridge and track leading to Colyford. As yet without overhead.** *Photograph Geoff Tribe.*

**Overhead erection went on while much needed revenue was earned by battery running.** *Seaton Tramway collection.*

**Car 2 at Colyford, showing the single stub end track and details of the battery trailer.** *Photograph Geoff Tribe.*

**Detail of car 2, with the legal lettering showing Claude Lane as General Manager.** *Photograph Geoff Tribe.*

**Car 2 at Colyford in the days of battery operation, with a good number of customers.** *Photograph Geoff Tribe.*

realisation of Claude's dreams.

In 1974 Cyril Chaplyn was invited to join the Board of Directors and he continued to be a Board member until his retirement in 1984.

## An Opportunity to Reach the Car Park

Part of the original plan was to extend the line from the depot around Warner's Holiday Camp to the public car park. This part of the line had been included in the Light Railway Order. However, difficulties over land purchase had meant that a section of line would have to be built on concrete piles in order to carry the rails above a stream. This would have incurred vast cost. After the death of Claude a neighbouring farmer approached Allan and offered a strip of land to the tramway. With this land the extension could be laid without the need for the expensive piles. This offer was gratefully accepted and the purchase went ahead. The terminus was to be on an eight feet wide strip on the edge of the car park. It was to have two stub sidings, one to take the tram shop.

The expense and time commitment in relaying the track meant that it was not possible to erect overhead in 1972. So the opportunity was taken to modify the rail. It had been supplied in 30 feet lengths and during this year the rail was welded in pairs to give 60 feet lengths. The new trackwork was inspected by Lt-Col Townsend Rose from the Railway Inspectorate in March 1973 and accepted. During 1972 a new type of passenger started visiting the tramway. The line runs along the estuary of the River Axe that, with its marshy islands and tidal quality, forms a natural sanctuary for all kinds of wading and sea birds. An amazing 53 varieties have been noted in just one day. Bird watchers soon found that a ride on the tramcars gave an excellent vantage point to watch the wild life. It was suggested by some of the naturalists that a tram would make an ideal mobile hide from which to observe the birds. A trial ride was planned for a Sunday morning, before the regular service. It proved a great success and for many years a special bird watching tram was run once a month. It stopped every few hundred yards and the passengers would use binoculars to spot the different varieties of birds. Often specialist groups and Societies would charter a tram. Indeed the Seaton representative of the Royal Society for the Protection of Birds had a special season ticket that permitted him to stop a tramcar at any point on the line to join or leave it. The tradition of running bird watching specials outside the normal operating hours has continued through to the present day.

## Overhead Operation at Last

1972 saw the main erection of overhead traction poles. 79 traction poles were needed and most of the poles had been purchased in 1970 from the Eastbourne Corporation Lighting Department, with a few from Bournemouth and some of the home-made poles from the Eastbourne tramway. The overhead fittings (insulators, hangers, ears and frogs) were purchased from Bradford Corporation when its trolleybus system was closed (the last in the country). At the same time they purchased trolleybus skids from Bradford and subsequently fitted them to all the trams. The carbon insert skids are quieter than the trolley wheels previously used.

The traction poles were set up at 40 yard intervals on the straight track and closer on curves, loops and points. Each pole is set in a three feet deep hole in a firm concrete mix. When the poles started to be erected an officer from the Council contacted the tramway and said that they would need to get agreement from the Council on the colour of paint used on the poles and on the depot doors. An official called around and Allan suggested that most tramways used green paint on the traction poles and it was a colour that would blend into the rural nature of the line. He also suggested that the depot doors could be painted the same colour. The Council gave their formal approval and so the traction poles and the doors were painted green. Many years later, when the depot was extended, Allan thought that a change of colour for the doors would be nice. So he contacted the Council to ask if he could change the colour of the doors. They came back to ask why they were being contacted about colours, it was

**A view of Colyford from car 2 showing the old railway level crossing gates at the road that formed a barrier for many years.** *Photograph Geoff Tribe.*

**Car 8 on the depot curve.** *Seaton Tramway collection.*

**Car 14 under construction in the depot.** *Photograph Geoff Tribe.*

**Cars 2 and 8 at the depot terminus during battery operation days.** *Photograph Geoff Tribe.*

**Sid Coates conducts car 7, with car 12 also in service at the depot terminus.** *Seaton Tramway collection.*

nothing to do with them and he could paint the doors whatever colour he liked!

All the traction poles from the depot to Colyford had been erected by early 1973 and new ¼-inch diameter copper wire from BICC was installed. Another task that was necessary before the line could be opened for electrical operation was to ensure that all the rail joints were electrically connected by welding bonding wires across the joints and putting heavy electrical wires along the track to feed the different sections of the overhead. The power was generated by a 26HP Robson diesel in the depot building which drove two Lister dynamos, one for the overhead DC and the other for the AC supply to the workshops. As with the other tramways, batteries were used as a reserve when there was high demand and in emergency should the generator fail. A second sub station was built in a former gangers' concrete hut between the Axmouth Loop and Bobsworth Bridge. This supplied current for the section from Bobsworth Bridge to Colyford. In the hut they installed a new DC Lister diesel generator. This was switched on by the first driver in the morning and off by the last driver in the evening. On Sunday 23rd September 1973 the first tramcar to carry passengers using the overhead power ran from the depot to Colyford. It was actually a special car commissioned by London members of the Light Railway Transport League.

An unusual episode occurred in 1974. In the June the overhead railway specialists Brecknell Willis approached the tramway. They had developed a single arm pantograph and were looking for somewhere to run tests on it. British Railways were interested in the idea, but needed to have a proven product. They could not afford to have main lines blocked by failed experimental pantographs. While test tracks could have been used, what Brecknell Willis wanted was operational use. The tramway agreed to undertake the trials. Obviously the open top tramcars were not suitable for the trials, so number 12 was fitted with the pantograph and used it during the normal operations of

**Car 8 at Colyford terminus.** *Photograph Geoff Tribe.*

**Cars 2 and 8 at the depot terminus, with 02 and a tipper wagon leaving for more tracklaying.** *Seaton Tramway collection.*

the tramway. They soon found it was necessary to extend the contact pan as the overhead was erected for trolley pole operation and in some places was not over the centre of the track. By adding an extension it ensured that the pan did not lose contact with the wire. Another Brecknell Willis pantograph to the same design was fitted to tram number 4. Although number 4 is an open car it has a short covered central section and this was suitable for fitting the pantograph. The pantographs performed well in the trials and the design has been used on new main line electric locomotives, running express trains at over 100mph. Something not attained by numbers 4 or 12!

## The Extension to the Car Park

This now allowed the organisation to focus on the extension to the car park. Strips of land had been purchased from a local farmer and this was combined with a lease from the council for a strip of land adjacent to the holiday camp. A Ruston and Hornsby Diesel 0-4-0 locomotive was purchased from the North Devon Clay Company at Torrington along with some tip wagons from a china clay works near Corfe Castle. The locomotive had to have several tons of ballast weights removed and be regauged from 3 feet to 2 feet 9 inches before it could be used. Then it set to work. A long ramp had to be built from the field level up a slope of 1 in 40 to the old railway embankment. To construct this they bought brick rubble from a local brick factory. A total of one thousand tons was used, all having to be transported from either the

**Car 4 at an extended Colyford.** *Seaton Tramway collection.*

car park or the depot to the ramp, with no road access. A temporary works line was laid to allow the diesel to move the rubble in the tip wagons. In addition two substantial bridges had to be built over drainage dykes. The Council offered reinforced concrete beams from the old station and these were used as the longitudinal members of the bridges. Steel beams were used as transverse bearing members. The land around this area

**Cars 4 and 8 on service at Colyford, with 02 parked in the stub siding. The Victorian gents urinal is the only part of the original railway station that survives.** *Seaton Tramway collection.*

**Allan and Sue Gardner on car 2 in the depot.** *Seaton Tramway collection.*

**Laying track at Poppy Corner on the extension to the car park.** *Seaton Tramway collection.*

**The first track reaches the car park allowing the trams to be easily seen by the public.** *Seaton Tramway collection.*

is marshy and poorly drained, so the ramp was given transverse land drains as it was built. For roughly half the length the 30 lb per yard ex-Sierra Leone rail was used and on the other half some of the 20 lb per yard rail from the Eastbourne tramway was utilised. For the overhead wire some heavier gauge wire from Bradford was used. As the adjacent fields were used for grazing cattle it was essential to erect a stout fence to keep the animals away from the line. Though they were very docile, their friendliness would be an embarrassment if they wandered on to the track.

**Opening Day of the extension to the car park.** *Seaton Tramway collection.*

The extension line at the depot leads through a tight right angle curve over a bridge. Then it goes down the ramp, along a straight line to the end of the holiday camp grounds, where it turns another tight right angle to run along the side of the car park. After a short distance another two sharp right angle turns take the line to the side of the car park. Here the terminus had two stub ends with an integral passing loop to allow the tram shop to be parked at the end. The shop had no motors so was towed behind the first tram of the day. It was parked close to the terminal traction pole where it was plugged into the power. Many of the tight curves on the extension are blind, owing to hedgerows. So for safety that part of the line has always been run on a staff system. That is a system where there is a special staff, a piece of painted wood, for the drivers. No tram is allowed on that section of the line unless the driver either has the staff, or has seen the staff, just before entering the section. This makes sure that no tram will meet another coming the other way. This is not required on the other single track sections of the line because the drivers can see a long distance along the track and can easily stop before meeting an oncoming tram. The system used ensures that trams only meet at the proper passing loops. In addition to the staff system there is radio communication along the whole of the line, so that the drivers are immediately informed of any unusual situation.

The extension was officially opened on Sunday 17th May 1975, with number 12 being the first tramcar, followed by number 8. This allowed the full season to be run to see how much effect the extension had on the number of passengers. As predicted by Claude, the extension to the car park was the key to the whole of the operation of the tramway. The results were dramatic with the total

**The complete terminus showing the proximity of the car parking area.** *Seaton Tramway collection.*

**Plenty of passengers board car 2 for a ride to Colyford.** *Seaton Tramway collection.*

**Plenty of customers on a hot sunny day, showing how much more attention the tramway got at its new terminus.** *Seaton Tramway collection.*

**Car 02 brings back the tram shop 01 at the end of a day's operation.** *Seaton Tramway collection.*

**Car 02, the tram shop, in detail.**

number of passengers rising sharply to 36,000, for the public the tramway was now visible from the roadway and as they parked their cars it was obviously a very tempting attraction.

Tickets were sold from the mobile tramshop 01, in its same role as at Eastbourne. That is a ticket shop and a place for visitors to buy souvenirs of the tramway. The difference between Seaton and Eastbourne was that the tramshop had its motors removed at Seaton and so it was towed to the car park each morning. The tramshop gave sterling service until the new terminus was constructed in 1995.

## Across the Road to Colyton

Completion of the car park extension now allowed the company to move forward to the fourth and final stage of the plan. This was the extension to Colyton. Approval had already been given in the Light Railway Order for traffic lights to be placed on the level crossing on the A3052, Lyme Regis to Sidmouth road. Preparations began and rail and sleepers prepared. The first large job was to lay the tramway across the road. Arrangements were made with the highway authorities and the police to close the road one night so they could work uninterrupted. The date set was 15th November 1975. A gang of workers and volunteers were assembled at Colyford on a wet and miserable evening. The road was closed and at 11.30pm they started to dig out the old British Rail track. This was a hefty 90 lb per yard rail, which had to be man-handled out of the way. The grooved tram rail (from the old Sheffield Corporation Tramways) was laid at 2 feet 9 inches gauge. The discomfort of the night was relieved by trips to car 12, which had been parked at Colyford as a soup kitchen and sheltered rest area. There was one incident during the night. Having opened up the road and removed the old rail a car arrived wanting to go into Colyford. Allan explained the situation and said the car would have to go via Colyton. But the driver had been imbibing and suggested that he could just drive across the excavation. Allan recommended that he did not, but the driver was impatient and revved up his engine. Allan cleared everyone away and the car shot across the road works. All went well until the car reached the step out of the excavation. The front wheels made it easily, but the exhaust did not. With a screeching sound the whole of the exhaust became detached from the car and rolled to the side of the road. The driver halted on the other side, got out his car and surveyed the damage. With many threats of suing the tramway for the damage and a very loud car, he went home. The only consequence was a local resident who was very embarrassed each time he saw Allan.

The gang finalised the track and resurfaced the road so that by 8.00am the road was re-opened and ready for traffic. This small part of the line had links to some of the earliest tramway legislation. In 1870 the Tramways Act was passed which was aimed at making it easier for tramways to be built. One section of the Act related to the responsibility of the tramway in the upkeep of the roads they had track in. The Act was written when horse trams were in the majority, so Parliament decreed that the tramway was responsible for the upkeep of the road surface between the rails and for eighteen inches each side. It was considered that the horses hauling the trams would wear out the road not only between the rails, but they could easily wander either side and so the tramway had to look after the road surface for an extra eighteen inches either side. This onerous and expensive responsibility stayed in the Act even though horses were replaced by electric motors that meant that the wheels only ran on the rails and never got near the road surface. So Modern Electric Tramways has to pay for the up-keep of a stretch of road surface 4 feet 3 inches wide across the road.

So track laying from Colyford to Colyton was now a practical proposition. During the winter of 1975/1976 a mile of track was laid. Until the traffic lights were erected, some years later, the works trams would reach the road and one of the crew would need to stop traffic using hand signals to allow the tram to cross. As much existing material as possible was recycled. So the old ballast from the railway line was used for the tramway. However, in 1968 a bad flood of the River Coly had washed off much of the ballast on the section north of Colyford. This meant that the track-layers had to recover the ballast from the brambles alongside the track. Not a pleasant task because it all had to be done by hand. Work continued in the winter of 1976/1977 and 35 traction poles were erected.

In 1976 the council built a large hut to house a Youth Club just beyond the Seaton terminus. This effectively hid the trams from the road, though they were still visible from the car park. But it did have an impact on passing trade. Representations to the council were met by the explanation that a space had been left between the Youth Centre hut and the fence so that the tramway could be extended to end at the road. However, this was thwarted in 1978 when a large toilet block was built behind the Youth Club and butting against the fence, cutting off any thought of extending the tramway to the road.

On 1st October 1978 the tramway system in Hamburg ceased running. It was unusual for

**A line up of cars 8, 7 and 6 at Riverside.** *Seaton Tramway collection.*

**Car 7 at Colyford, track is about to be laid across the road to open the way to Colyton.** *Photograph John H Meredith.*

**Car 01 the tram shop as rebuilt to allow more display space for the souvenirs and tram books on sale.** *Photograph Daniel Hill.*

**Cars 7 and 01 at the car park terminus.**

**Cars 17, 16 and 12 in the depot.** *Seaton Tramway collection.*

**Sue Gardner driving 4 on a busy day.** *Seaton Tramway collection.*

a German tramway of that time because it used trolley pole current collection and not the more common pantograph. Allan contacted them and arranged for the purchase of a variety of fittings, particularly trolley poles, including bases and heads. Allan had already had experience of the Hamburg tramway when, twenty years earlier, he had been posted near there when doing his National Service. He often went to see the tramway and was just getting to know the tramway staff when he was moved to another part of Germany and was unable to make a closer relationship. So he had pleasure in going back to see the system, but this was tinged with sadness because of the demise of the tramway. He drove to Hamburg to collect the items. When he arrived he asked whereabouts his purchases were, only to be told to help himself to anything he wanted. The car was filled and trolley arms were strapped to the roof rack. The long drive back along the autobahns was accomplished without problems and then onto the ferry. As he drove off the ferry and queuing to go through customs, the driver of a car alongside wound down its window and shouted "I know where you are going with that lot! You're off to the National Tram Museum at Crich". Allan took delight in replying "No, we are off to the Seaton Tramway".

Everything was ready in 1978 for

**Track laying from Colyford to Colyton.** *Seaton Tramway collection.*

the installation of the traffic lights. But then the River Coly burst its banks again and flooded the area, removing some newly laid ballast. The South West Water Authority decided to install extensive flood defence measures in the area. This included changing the road layout, so delaying installation of the traffic lights. They could not be installed until the winter of 1979/1980. Again the tramway is responsible for the cost and upkeep of the lights. With the lights in place the tramway was ready to open the extension. The Ministry of Transport inspected the line on 3rd March 1980 and approved the line. Public service started on 8th March 1980.

The operation of the traffic lights is incorporated into the standing instructions to all drivers. The driver approaches the crossing and halts at the stop board before the road is reached. Here there is a plunger, protected by a key. The driver needs to leave the tramcar, then check the road and if there is traffic they must wait for a lull. Then they unlock and press the plunger, getting back into the tram as the lights operate. A flashing amber light operates for eight seconds to warn and stop the road traffic. Then twin flashing red lights are operated indicating that all road traffic must stop. When the driver has the clear signal, they drive carefully across the road, checking for traffic. At the other side there is a treadle on the track that is operated when the wheels of the tram go across it. This switches off the flashing lights. In fact there are two sets of treadles on the Colyford side because there are two tracks immediately after the crossing.

## Colyton Station

The old station building at Colyton was still standing, though in the original transaction it was not included in the purchase of the line. Maurice Jones, a retired signalman at Seaton Junction, and his wife were tenants of the Station Master's House and the rest of the station building. Later British

**Cars 6, 8 and 01 at the car park terminus.** *Seaton Tramway collection.*

**Colyford in the early days with the Ruston diesel in use.** *Seaton Tramway collection.*

**Car 2 crossing the road at Colyford.** *Photograph authors.*

**Looking back from Colyton at the new track.** *Seaton Tramway collection.*

**Sue and Allan Gardner on the Ruston diesel.** *Seaton Tramway collection.*

**Construction of the new terminus at Colyton.** *Seaton Tramway collection.*

**Car 7 in the early days of Colyton terminus.** *Seaton Tramway collection.*

Railways approached the tramway company to ask if they were interested in purchasing the building, but with the tenants in place. The company was keen and visited Mr and Mrs Jones to discuss the purchase. They found the couple very worried, because they had heard about the offer and were concerned that they would be asked to leave. Allan assured them that they could stay in the house as long as they wanted. But they would have the trams running into the station. Mr and Mrs Jones said that they were used to railway trains, so trams were no problem. With everyone satisfied the purchase went ahead for just £1,700. In 1997 Mr and Mrs Jones decided that they needed to move into a bungalow and Allan helped them find a suitable place. This left the station building empty. At this time Allan and Sue were looking for somewhere else to live. So they moved into the building in 1978.

With the opening of the line to Colyton the tramway had reached the full extent envisaged by Claude Lane. He had planned four stages, stage one being the initial line from the depot to Bobsworth Bridge, second the extension to Colyford. Then the opening of the line to the car park near Harbour Road and finally the crossing of the A3052 and the line to Colyton. The tramway was complete just ten years after the granting of the Light Railway Order and the first trams moved on to the site from Eastbourne.

**Colyton station buildings, at this time used by Allan and Sue Gardner as their home. It was also a storage area for some works trailers.** *Seaton Tramway collection.*

# CHAPTER 6

# Developments on the Seaton Tramway

A chance meeting occurred in 1981 when Eric Thornton, a retired Works Manager and tramway enthusiast, visited Seaton and the tramway. To cut a long story short, Eric was asked to join the tramway Board and this proved a very valuable partnership for six years. Eric was born in Bradford and was very knowledgeable about tramway practice as well as a superb tramway model engineer. He was able to provide a level of both management and engineering expertise that the tramway urgently needed. He and Allan Gardner worked well together and his contribution was such that he was invited to become a Director of the company, until his second retirement in 1986. Also in 1981 Fred Wallace, the brother in law to Roger Lane, became a Director and joined the Board.

### Colyton Improvements

With the line fully opened, the focus of attention turned to developing and improving the facilities and tramcars. Indeed for the first year of operation to Colyton there were no facilities at the terminus for passengers. After the ride to Colyton passengers would often alight and make the short walk to the town centre. Allan had further plans for the terminus. He wanted to take the line left, down the embankment to the road level. It was then to go under the bridge and back up the station driveway. Here it would connect with the line back to Seaton. This would have provided a turning loop, though not for passengers. The idea was that the trams would empty at the station, travel around the loop and back to the station for loading. The real reason for the loop would have been to provide a connection to the road so that a spur could be built that would link the station with the town. But this was not to be and the tramway remained on the station site.

Soon after the extension was opened the parish council wrote to the tramway to ask them to provide toilets at the terminus. So the old station toilets were refurbished and re-opened. Colyton gained some facilities in 1981 when Fred Wallace opened a mobile tea bar at the end of the line. Fred continued to provide this service until 1984 when Alan Williams took on the tea bar. Alan had been running a cafe and model

**The gang lifting the Torquay track in 1984 in the old St Mary Church depot. From left to right, Allan Gardner, Alan Williams, Ron Hubble and David Chaplyn.** *Photograph Alan Williams.*

**Loosening the setts around the point rails.** *Photograph Alan Williams.*

**Setts removed and the point rails exposed, ready for loading on to the lorry.** *Photograph Alan Williams.*

**The point blades exposed and ready to go.** *Photograph Alan Williams.*

**Members of the TLRS on a special visit inspect the reconstruction of car 12.** *Photograph authors.*

tramway shop in Torquay. While there he had contacted Allan to tell him about some old track that survived from the old Torquay Tramways. Arrangements were made for the rails and a point to be removed from the works yard where they were. Allan and a team from Seaton went to Torquay and were joined by Alan Williams. The rails were lifted and the road surface relaid (the owners of the works gave the rail provided the surface was reinstated). The rails were taken to Seaton and the straights were used in the depot while the point was laid at Colyton in 1985 as part of the development of the station area. It can be seen today, as the very last point on the line.

The developments at Colyton in 1985 were external. The upper end of the track was paved over and a more attractive boarding area was built. At this time Alan Williams was keen to become a volunteer at Seaton. So he left Torquay and moved into a flat in Seaton. He took over the Colyton tea bar. It was agreed that Alan could use the former waiting room for his model tram layout and shop. He renovated the room and built a tramway layout to demonstrate his tramway products. A colleague ran the tea bar and the shop became mainly a mail order business, which allowed Alan to pursue his first love which was to drive tramcars. This arrangement continued until 1986 when Alan moved to Birmingham.

**Cars 2 and 4 at Colyton with Alan Williams' tea bar in the background.** *Seaton Tramway collection.*

When the majority of the work on the Colyton extension was completed, the company was now able to focus on the tramcars. Work on the trams had been reduced to essential maintenance during the development period. The first task was to attend to number 12. Completed in 1966, it had been needing an overhaul since 1976. So in the winter of 1978/79 an extensive rebuilding of the tramcar was started. First it was lengthened and the saloon changed to a design more like that of the other tramcars. Then the tram was given staircases and an open top, upper deck. It was virtually a new tram that emerged from the workshops in 1980. It had become the highest capacity tram in the fleet, with seating for 45 passengers.

In the winter of 1981 a fierce gale blew over works car 02. The body was badly damaged, well beyond patching up. It was necessary to rebuild the body completely. The tramway decided to use the opportunity to enlarge the platforms and build hexagonal dashes. The motor bogies were removed and lightweight trailer bogies fitted. This meant that the car had to be towed out to work on the overhead. However, at this time there was little other than routine maintenance to do.

## New Trams from Old

Once number 12 was back in service the workshop had sufficient capacity to look at building a new tramcar. Of course there was one just waiting to be finished. The body of Metropolitan Electric Tramways number 94 had been at Eastbourne since 1961, when it had been agreed that a group of enthusiasts could store and work on the tramcar in the tramway workshops. This was a massive project and work progressed very slowly. So in 1968 the group donated the body to Modern Electric Tramways. Claude had decided to use the body to make a new tram, but it had to be narrowed by cutting a section out of the bulkheads and joining the sides back together. The move to Seaton delayed completion of the tram and it was not until 1980 that work could recommence. A clerestory roof was constructed, giving the tramcar a period design. It was painted in a red and white livery, like that carried by the tram in its former days. The controllers

**Not quite fully painted, the rebuilt car 12 is pressed into service.** *Seaton Tramway collection.*

**The finished tramcar resplendent in its new livery.** *Photograph Daniel Hill.*

**Car 14 standing on the depot fan in 1985.** *Photograph Alan Pearce.*

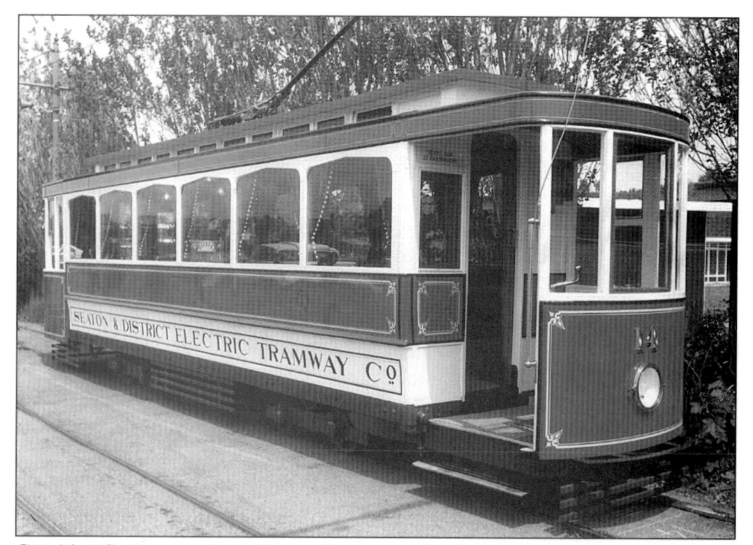

**Car 14 at Seaton terminus.** *Seaton Tramway collection.*

**Car 17 on the depot fan, temporarily on trucks borrowed from 4 with the construction crew, left to right, Allan Gardner, Sue Gardner, Geoff Sawford, Keith Marlow, Dave Saunders, Dave Chaplyn and Len Watts.** *Seaton Tramway collection.*

**Car 17 in use with driver Denis Higgs helping a wheelchair passenger up the ramp. The new platforms at Seaton and Colyton now makes access much easier.** *Seaton Tramway collection.*

came second-hand from Lisbon. These created somewhat of a fuss. They had been purchased through the London office of the Lisbon tramway. When they arrived in England they passed into the hands of the Customs and Excise. The controllers puzzled Customs and they were unsure what duty to charge. So a member of the Customs visited the tramway. He asked what the controllers were for and was shown the trams running on the line and the body of 14. He then asked if there was any intention to import a large number of controllers for resale. He was assured that this was a one off. It was decided that no excise duty would be payable.

Using the lower saloon sides of a full size tramcar has meant that number 14 is very large compared to previous Seaton trams. Indeed the roof comes higher than the upper deck railings of the open top tramcars. The tram was completed in 1984 and television personality Larry Grayson was asked to perform the inaugural ceremonies in June. He was asked to say a few words and then drive the tram away from the car park terminus. He was so captivated by the tramway that he wanted to continue driving for the rest of the day. He had even managed to get a motorman's cap and quite looked the part.

Tram 14 proved a great success. It was the most comfortable of all the trams, with upholstered and padded seats and even curtains at the windows. It proved that large trams were very practical on the tramway. So the company set about resolving a problem that had been growing in size. The number of visitors using wheelchairs had been increasing. The tramway always did what it could to accommodate such visitors, helping the more able to get into the lower seats of the trams. But on some occasions large groups would arrive. So it was decided that a larger size of single deck tram could be used to advantage for carrying wheelchairs. Thus number 17 was designed. Allan decided to base the design on the cross bench tramcars running on the Manx Electric Railway on the Isle of Man. The open sided design gives good access for wheelchairs, while the seats were designed to be easily removable, while Eric Thornton designed the trucks. Construction of the tramcar started in December 1987 and it was completed in just three months, ready for the start of the 1988 season. When finished the tram was able to seat 48 passengers and is particularly popular on sunny days. When all the removable seats are taken out, the tram will take 12 wheelchair passengers with 10 helpers. Generally the demand is for one or two wheelchairs to be carried. The staff can quickly remove a seat or two, put on the portable ramps, carried at all times by the tram, the wheelchair passengers board the tram and the wheelchairs are secured using clamps in slots built into the floor of the tram. The tram has proved extremely useful and of course very popular with both wheelchair bound and able bodied visitors.

**The bodies of Bournemouth 31 and 106 after delivery to Riverside.** *Seaton Tramway collection.*

**Car 106 was selected for rebuilding into car 16. Here construction is at an advanced stage, with Allan Gardner working on it.** *Seaton Tramway collection.*

## Back at Colyton

In 1986 Dave and Maggs Saunders took over management of the ground floor of Colyton station. They converted the model tram shop into a tea room and set up another room as a small souvenir shop. These proved very popular with visitors and the shop gradually built up to have a much larger range of items than the tram shop 01 could offer. This demonstrated the potential for additional income from souvenir sales as well as refreshments. Plans were made for further development at Colyton.

In 1988 the number of passengers using the tramway rose to 79,000. Numbers 14 and 17 had proved very successful so it was decided to undertake another conversion. The company had some other old tram bodies and ex-Bournemouth tramcar number 106 was selected as the next project. This tram was built in 1921 and had run in Bournemouth until the system closed in 1936. Some of its sister cars had been sold to the L&CBER to continue in service, but number 106 had been stripped of all its equipment and the body sold and moved to Kinson. Here it was saved by the Bournemouth Transport Preservation Group. The Group also had number 85, which had been sold to the L&CBER. The Group had restored it for exhibiting in their now closed transport museum. It is now in the Museum of Electricity, Christchurch. They have a number of other tram bodies, but all in store requiring extensive renovation. So in 1974 number 106 was passed on to Seaton. Conversion of the body started in 1988. Like number 14 a section was taken out of the bulkheads to narrow the tramcar. While 14 was cut down to 5 feet 4 inches, the company followed its usual tradition of making new trams bigger than the previous ones, so the Bournemouth car was made 5 feet 9 inches wide. It was fitted with a clerestory roof. The finished tram was painted in the Bournemouth livery of deep maroon and primrose. A decision had already been taken to number the tramcar 16, reflecting the original number and still fitting in with the other fleet numbers. The transfers for the lettering, the corner motifs for the lining and the crests were all produced by Stan Letts. This is described in more detail in Appendix 1. It was decided on this car that the usual practice of putting two crests on each side (one for Modern Electric Tramways and one for Seaton and District Tramway) would not suit number 16. So different crests were put on each side. This led to a redesign of the crests, which is detailed in Appendix 1. The tram entered service in 1991.

Having completed three new trams over the past seven years the workshops turned their attention to the existing fleet. Number 6, now 35 years old and the oldest tram in the fleet, was brought in for a rebuild. It had been decided to remove the small lower deck saloons that had been fitted in 1962 and replace them with cross bench seating, bringing it back to its original 1956 design. This was done to improve the ride for passengers. There were two advantages in removing the saloon. There was more leg room for passengers and they would get a better view from the tramcar. Once back in service it became clear that passengers enjoyed the full cross bench design. So in 1992 number 8 was rebuilt in the same way.

**The completed car 16 ready to go into service.** *Seaton Tramway collection.*

## Further Strengthening of the Management Team

For several years from the mid 1970s Brian Horner and Trevor Shears had been spending increasing amounts of time at Seaton as volunteers. Both were senior managers of major bus companies and Brian was chairman of the North York Moors Railways. It was appreciated that with Cyril Chapman's and Eric Thornton's retirements the Board needed strengthening. In December 1989 both Brian and Trevor were invited to join the Board and have remained very active members ever since. Indeed Brian became Chairman and Trevor Company Secretary. Their contribution and vision on further development of the tramway has been fundamental to the creation of the highly successful tourist attraction seen today.

**Car 16 goes into service.** *Photograph John H Meredith.*

## Moving Closer to Seaton Town Centre

1992 was also the year that thoughts turned to making the tramway more visible to passing tourists at the Seaton end. Allan approached the Council with proposals to extend the terminus by turning across the end of the Youth Club and turning again to end near the road. The Council were considering improvements to the road layout in that part of the town so deferred the proposals. Discussions continued with the Council and it was agreed that a piece of land could be used for the new terminus. This meant that the track layout is unusual and more cramped than the Company would

**The major feature of the terminus is the shop. The frame is erected.** *Seaton Tramway collection.*

have preferred. The Company commissioned the John Home Design Practice as architects and a striking, but traditional, building was designed. Modern Electric Tramways funded the whole of the building works, including the building, trackwork and paving block laying.

The new track-work had to be laid without interrupting the normal service. Two points were placed in the outer stub line and this allowed track to be laid giving a curving loop in front of the new terminal building, which come together to a single stub end easily visible from the road. To emphasise the attraction a period style cast iron sign announcing "Electric Tramway" goes over the walkway leading to the terminus building. 1995 was the Silver Jubilee of the Seaton Tramway, the purchase of the old track bed having been completed on 3rd May, so there were special celebrations during that month. But events were also planned throughout the year, so the opportunity was taken to have an official opening of the new terminus during the August events. The month started with an Enthusiasts weekend, then on 28th came the

**Lisbon 730 stored at Colyton, with 6 in service.** *Photograph John H Meredith.*

**Contractors prepare the new terminus at Seaton.** *Seaton Tramway collection.*

**The completed shop and covered waiting area, showing the attractive design in keeping with the period atmosphere of the tramway.** *Photograph John Meredith.*

Silver Jubilee of Seaton as a passenger carrying tramway. In 1995 this was the August Bank Holiday Monday. So to allow the new terminus to be used for the whole of the holiday weekend it was officially opened on Saturday 26th.

The new road layout set out by the council meant that a new relief road was built that runs next to the new terminus, giving passers-by a superb view of the tramway.

For the Silver Jubilee tramcar number 8 was repainted in a striking yellow and white livery and lettered "Silver Jubilee" on the decency panels and "1970 – 1995" on the ends. It was prominent in the festivities celebrating the anniversary.

In the winter of 1995/96 more work was done at Colyton. In the January the old platform wall and station garden was removed and a new toilet block erected. New gable ends were built onto the station roof in readiness for a prefabricated canopy. New fencing was put along the platform edge. The track was replaced, using some more of the Torquay rails that were lifted and moved in 1984. The whole of the track in front of the platform was given a typical period street surface of setts. The improved terminus was ready for the 1996 season.

## The Depot

With both termini rebuilt building work moved to the depot. For many years the workshop had suffered from a lack of storage space, so planning permission was obtained to construct a two storey store at the back of the depot. This was completed in 1996. At the same time it was realised that additional space was needed

**In 1995, when the tramway celebrated its Silver Jubilee, car 8 was painted in a striking yellow livery with appropriate lettering.** *Photograph John H Meredith.*

**Car 8 in its Jubilee livery at Colyford.** *Photograph John H Meredith.*

**Car 16 at the refurbished Colyton terminus. The full block paving looks most attractive.** *Seaton Tramway collection.*

**Another view of car 16 and the newly refurbished Colyton terminus.** *Seaton Tramway collection.*

for new tramcars, so plans were put in motion for a forty foot extension and restyled front. The John Home Design Practice were commissioned again to style the extension and the area in front of the depot. Allan had seen some photographs of the tram depot at Halle, Germany and suggested that some of the features could be incorporated. Of course the iron gates from Hendon had to be included. The extension was the usual style of factory building, but the end was to be clad in traditional brick to give an older look. Outside the yard was given a brick wall with railings that complement the gates. The railings were purchased second-hand from Axminster station and goods yard.

**The extension to the station building blends in well with the original design.** *Seaton Tramway collection.*

## 1996 Llandudno Festival of Transport

A Festival of Transport was first organised in Llandudno over the May Day weekend in 1993, using Bodafon Fields, through which the original Llandudno and Colwyn Bay Electric Railway ran. For the May Day Festival in 1996 the organiser, Len Ricketts, felt it would be appropriate to display a tramcar as part of the Festival, as it was the 40th anniversary of the closure of the tramway (the last tram having carried passengers on 24th April 1956).

Len contacted the owners of a number of preserved trams without any success. Then he spoke to Allan Gardner who agreed to loan number 6 for the period of the festival. Later when Len asked Allan why he had not put the phone down on the idea, like the other tramcar owners, Allan replied that the late Claude Lane would have wanted to listen and would certainly have agreed to number 6 going to Llandudno. It was the first of the 'Eastbourne' design of tramcars, which were loosely based on the L&CBER ex-Bournemouth trams and number 6 itself has upper deck seats and mesh from the L&CBER.

Number 6 was a very appropriate choice. It had started its life as an open toastrack tramcar built to run on the 15-inch gauge track at Voryd Park, Rhyl, just a short distance

**The full impact of the terminus is best seen from the front of an open top tram entering the station.** *Photograph authors.*

**Cars 2 and 7 on a sunny summer's day with the tramway well patronised.** *Photograph authors.*

**Car 6 being unloaded from the lorry at Llandudno onto the temporary track.** *Photograph Daniel Hill.*

**Car 6 at Llandudno, only able to be displayed as a static exhibit.** *Photograph Daniel Hill.*

**Behind car 6 are the other attractions at the Llandudno Festival of Transport.** *Photograph Daniel Hill.*

from Llandudno. When it was rebuilt as an open top car for running at Eastbourne it was given top deck seats, wire mesh, headlights and gongs all from the old Llandudno tramway system.

The intention was to carry passengers over a length of temporary track about 300 yards long. The proposal was very reminiscent of the old fête days in 1949 and 1950. No overhead was erected, instead batteries were to be used. The destination of the tramcar was set as "Service Extra". However, the festival organisers failed to contact the Health and Safety Executive to obtain the necessary approval. The Railway Inspectorate side of the HSE did not allow any passenger operation. To the disappointment of many the tramcar became a static exhibit. It was driven around the old Llandudno tram routes, unfortunately not under its own power, but being carried on the back of a lorry. It returned to Seaton after the festival.

## Television Appearance

In June 1996 the tramway was the subject of one episode of a series titled "Great Little Trains". This gave very welcome nationwide publicity for the tramway. The compère for the series was the television personality Willie Rushton. He enjoyed the filming and had a genuine interest in the tramway. So it was particularly saddening for all the tramway staff when they heard of his untimely death. It was made all the more poignant as the programme was broadcast only two weeks before his death.

## The Tramway Tribune

In the Summer of 1996 the tramway developed a new public relations venture. A newspaper, titled "The Tramway Tribune" was launched. Number 1 was dated Summer 1996, with the intention of printing a couple of issues each year to tell the public of the latest developments of the tramway and to feature archive material. The price was 40p and future issues would only be produced if there was sufficient interest.

# The Tramway Tribune

THE OFFICIAL NEWSPAPER OF SEATON & DISTRICT ELECTRIC TRAMWAY

*ISSUE 1, SUMMER 1996*

*40p*

**WELCOME to issue one of "The Tramway Tribune". This is a pilot issue which we hope will lead to a regular publication if enough interest is shown.**

We intend to publish news of the latest developments at Seaton Tramway, together with archive material, features and interviews with Tramway people. We also welcome any contributions such as photographs, articles, reminiscences or letters. If you would like to receive future editions, please register your interest by returning the cut-out slip on the back of this issue.

## *IMPROVED SERVICES IN 1996 - MORE DRIVERS RECRUITED*

***For the first time this year, Seaton Tramway has announced a twenty minute tram service on every day of the season, from April 1st right through until November 1st.***

*The service from Seaton will be 9.40am until 5.20pm, and from Colyton 10.10am until 5.50pm. An evening service will operate from July 20th until August 30th, with the last tram from Seaton at 8.40pm and the last from Colyton at 9.10pm. Also for the first time, we shall be running every day in October.*

*The increase in service has led to the recruitment of more seasonal part-time tram drivers; a total of ten will be working in the busy July/August period. This will allow the full time staff to tackle the ever-increasing amount of maintenance necessary. Not only does the company have to keep up regular servicing on the fleet of nine tramcars, but cutting grass, trees and brambles on the trackside is an on-going chore, as is track work, overhead work and keeping the new facilities at Seaton and Colyton properly cleaned and maintained. Despite the increase in paid staff, volunteer help is still very welcome and will continue to be an important part of the tramway.*

## REVAMPED COLYTON SPARKS NEW SEASON

**It was a race against time as the new season approached, but thanks to a big effort from all concerned the first service tram rolled into the revamped Colyton terminus at 10.03am on Good Friday, 5th April. This landmark was reached after an intense period of activity which began on January 15th when JCB's from Reg Lawrence Construction arrived to tear down the old platform wall and station house garden in order to dig foundations for the new toilet block. The existing track was removed and the ground levelled in preparation for relaying.**

The initial priority was to build 3 new gable ends onto the station roof in readiness for the arrival of the prefabricated canopy. Local carpenter Mark Harris, a veteran of the 1995 Seaton project, laboured hard to have this ready on time for the arrival of Andy Thornton's team from West Yorkshire. Thornton's assembled the canopy within 2 weeks, together with the fencing along the platform edge. Steve, Alex, Leroy and Greg worked very efficiently to finish the job on time and, as was the case in Seaton last year, were a credit to their firm.

Meanwhile Reg Lawrence's team pressed on with the new toilet block and also the levelling of the trackbed. Slots were dug for concrete sleepers along the length of the platform, and the Tramway's track gang led by Stuart Bright were then able to start laying track. Most of this section was relaid utilising grooved tram rail obtained from West Hill depot in Torquay on its demolition in 1984. After 60 years spent buried under tarmac it is once again being used for its true purpose! With the track down, stone sets were laid to complete the new "Street Tramway" appearance of the terminus.

The out bound track, which runs alongside the platform, is due for completion by the Spring Bank Holiday, and the first major test of the new layout will be on the occasion of the Bus Rally on Saturday 8th June. An official opening ceremony is being planned for later in the season, details to be announced.

**The first issue of The Tramway Tribune.**

**Footings start to be made for the depot extension.** *Photograph Alan Pearce.*

is a complex arrangement of overhead wires that enables the trolley pole to automatically turn at the terminus. It was not an essential fitting, but was done because the overhead linesmen wanted to take on the challenge.

The new facilities provided by the workshop and depot extension were put to good use immediately by putting number 2 into the new paintshop and giving a complete repaint.

An unfortunate reflection on today's society was apparent at the Seaton terminus building. It was necessary to replace all the glass in the building with a strong synthetic substitute. This was done to prevent the constant episodes of vandalism and broken glass in the building. In the winter of 1997/98 the track was relaid at the

## Depot Extension

Having obtained planning permission for the depot extension a start was made in the winter of 1996/97. Work started immediately the season finished on 1st November 1996. Not only was the forty foot extension to be built, but the existing building was to be given a new, warmer, roof. As usual the British weather had a hand in delaying the project. In February high winds twice blew down internal walls in the new offices, causing delays that also affected the re-roofing. The trams had to be stored at Colyton and were wrapped in tarpaulins to protect them as much as possible from the adverse weather conditions. The depot was able to be used for stabling trams by the beginning of the 1997 season.

A short while after the building had been completed they had a surprise visit from the county planning manager. He told Allan that he had driven into Seaton on the A358. Looking across the River Axe he had spotted the depot front and had called to complement the company on an excellent design, in keeping with the period charm of the tramway.

Despite the absence of a workshop, work on the construction of the rebuilding of Exeter 19 continued as best as possible.

In the Tramway Tribune number 3, published in April 1997 there was some speculation regarding the proposals to build three new trams. At the same time a trolley reverser had been installed at Colyton. This

**The floor of the extension is prepared as the framework of the building goes up around it.** *Photograph Alan Pearce.*

**A general view of the depot. The partitioned off area in the far right is the paint shop.** *Photograph authors.*

**The limited space means that complex point work is needed in the depot approach to enable the trams to take the correct road.** *Photograph authors.*

**The full depot fan, with Allan on the right.** *Photograph authors.*

**At the back of the depot there is still a memento of the very first days at Seaton. A small section of dual gauge track, used to unload trams from Eastbourne while they were still 2ft gauge.** *Photograph authors.*

**The full depot frontage which shows how sympathetically the building has been designed to blend in with the tramway.** *Photograph authors.*

depot curve. This was done to ease the sharp curve and at the same time the overhead on the curve and at the depot entrance was re-aligned.

## A Visitor from Abroad

In 1997 an unusual tramcar arrived at Seaton. The 900mm gauge tramway system in Lisbon, Portugal, were selling off their older four wheel tramcars and number 730 came to Seaton. As the gauge is only a few inches wider that Seaton's 2 feet 9 inches, it was felt that the tramcar might be able to be converted for use on the tramway. The tram was placed at the Colyton terminus, just the other side of the boundary wall. It was easily visited by passengers and many people viewed this foreign tramcar. Although it was built and ran in Portugal, the tramcar used an American design and it looked very

**On the right is the extension at the back of the depot, giving more, much needed, storage space.** *Photograph authors.*

**Lisbon 730 on tram jacks, with the truck removed.** *Photograph authors.*

different from the trams running into Colyton station.

## The Exeter Tram

In 1984 the body of an Exeter tramcar was discovered in Rewe and negotiations enabled it to be donated to the Mid Devon Tramway Preservation Society, an organisation set up to restore the tramcar to its former glory. The tram was number 19, built in 1906 as an open top four wheel tramcar. The car had been renumbered in 1929 becoming number 21. Unfortunately the preservation society were unable to take on the restoration project and the body was taken on by Colin Shears of the West of England Transport Collection, who then donated it to the Seaton Tramway in 1994. Following the success of numbers 14 and 16 it was decided to use the body to create a new tram for the fleet. As the number 19 fitted in well with existing trams it was kept. Like the previous conversions of full size bodies, the lower saloon had to have a section removed from the centre to narrow the width. As built the tramcar had a normal round dash, but in 1926 it was rebuilt and given a hexagonal dash. As no Seaton tram had this style of dash it was retained for 19.

The rebuilding of the tram was completed in 1998, with the tramcar being painted in the bright green and white Exeter livery. As Exeter is just down the road from Seaton there had been much interest expressed by the town during the restoration. So the tramway felt that the tramcar should be given a special official launch. Saturday 26th September was chosen and no less than 40 VIPs were invited to the launch. Number 19 had been placed at Seaton terminus and covered with a giant wrapper. The VIPs met at the Seaton Heights Hotel for a lunchtime reception, echoing the celebrations that were popular at the turn of the 19th century when new tramway systems were opened. Following a presentation on the development of the Seaton Tramway and its future aspirations the party was taken by coach to the Seaton terminus. Here the Chairman, Brian Horner, and the Managing Director, Allan Gardner, gave short speeches. The Mayor of Exeter, Councillor Barry McNamara then formally unveiled the tram and boarded to drive it to Riverside Depot. Here the party were shown the new extension and displays of the work of the tramway. Here Councillor

**Exeter 19 when it was in service.** *Seaton Tramway collection.*

Margaret Rogers, Chair of Devon County Council, cut a tape to officially inaugurate the depot. The party boarded number 19 again for a run to Colyton where a coach met the party to take them back to Seaton Heights.

The following day was an Enthusiasts Day. Number 19 ran in service getting many complimentary remarks about the quality of the work. During the day every available tramcar was brought in to service. So a nine car service was operated, number 14 being the only tram not able to be used as it was in the paint shop being repainted.

**Exeter 19 as found at Rewe, in need of some restoration.** *Photograph Ted Crawforth.*

## Honour from the Queen

In February 1998 Allan received an unexpected letter from Buckingham Palace informing him that he had been awarded the MBE for services to Seaton Tramway and tourism. After recovering from his shock he arranged with the Palace to attend the investiture on 26th November. Allan and Sue arranged to stay with friends in the South East and had the thrill of being driven through the gates of Buckingham Palace as honoured guests of the Queen. The policeman on duty stopped the car and had a chat with Allan, partly to tell him where he was to go and partly to relax him on such an important occasion. Allan was dressed in top hat and tails, a major change from the overalls used in the tram workshop. Then they were driven into the internal courtyard to the entrance to the Palace. Here Allan and Sue parted, with Allan going to join the other recipients of honours. Usually unruffled by any event, Allan admitted being over-

**On its official launch car 19 was literally kept under wraps until the Mayor of Exeter unveiled it.** *Photograph John H Meredith.*

**Car 19 stripped down and being rebuilt.** *Seaton Tramway collection.*

**The rebuilt car 19 in service for the first time with the Mayor driving it.** *Photograph John H Meredith.*

**Allan on the stairs in Buckingham Palace proudly shows his OBE.** *Seaton Tramway collection.*

whelmed by the experience. He found it daunting to be in the company of lords, knights and royalty. He was directed through large state rooms to congregate by the ballroom, where the investitures were to be held. A court officer then briefed them on what was to happen and informed everyone that the Queen was not able to conduct the ceremony herself that day owing to other commitments – she was entertaining the Emperor of Japan. It would be Prince Charles who would confer the honours.

When his turn came Allan walked up to the Prince and received his congratulations. The Prince admitted that he had not heard about the tramway before and he asked Allan about it. Allan reminded the Prince that his Great Grandfather had been the first person to drive an electric tram in London when he opened the LCC tramway in 1901. Allan said that the Prince would be most welcome to continue the family tradition at Seaton. Prince Charles expressed a great interest in visiting the tramway the next time he was in the area.

After the ceremony Allan said that the award reflected the efforts of all those who have helped the tramway over the years and it was wonderful that everyone's hard work should be recognised in this very public way. He was proud to have been honoured in this way and passed his congratulations to everyone.

## An Unusual Year

1998 was an unusual year for the tramway. It started poorly with extremely bad weather disrupting the transport rally in June and keeping visitor numbers down. Poor weather continued and depressed visitor numbers for the rest of June and July. Then the weather improved in August and it became a record month. The record for the busiest day was broken four times in just two weeks. Indeed the crowds were such that every tram was pressed into service to move people, particularly getting visitors back from Colyton, where queues of 80 or more were not unusual. One particularly pleasing aspect was the considerable increase in pre-booked group trips, forming part of a coach trip around the area. An unusual benefit from this is the practice of many coach firms to drop their passengers at Seaton terminus to be taken by tram to Colyton. Meanwhile the coach drives to Colyton to pick up the group. This allowed the tram to be placed in service to move other visitors back to Seaton. Over the year a record 83,000 passengers were carried.

The large numbers of visitors demonstrated that the gift shop at Colyton was getting too small to cope. So plans were put in place to double the area of the shop and possibly increase the kitchen and seating space in the Tea Rooms. But the improvements would have to wait until the year 2000.

## 30th Anniversary

The year 2000 not only saw the country celebrating the start of the new millennium, but was also the 30th anniversary of the Seaton Tramway. There was a good start with the 29th July seeing a new record on the

**Car 23 visits Seaton for the first time and shows just how small it is compared to the later trams. 12 is in service.** *Seaton Tramway collection.*

tramway. For the first time ever there were ten tramcars carrying passengers simultaneously. This came about because the tramway was running a busy six car service and had a pre-booked party of over 150 which required an additional four trams.

Tram number 8, which had been painted a special yellow and white livery for the 25th anniversary, was given a repaint in the same colours, but now with lettering suitable for the 30th Anniversary. In 1995 the 25th Anniversary was celebrated the whole year. The events included a special re-uniting of the first tramcar built by Claude Lane, number 23 and its newer brothers and sisters. The current owner of 23 took the tram to Seaton and it was displayed on the driveway of Colyton Station. As 23 is still in its 15-inch gauge condition it was not able to be operated on the tramway lines. But it was an opportunity to compare the extremely small nature of 23 (it was really built only for children), with the size of today's trams at Seaton.

## Another Tram Major Rebuild and More Work at Colyton

Later in the year 12 was taken into the depot for a major rebuilding programme. The largest change was to be the fitting of new ends, with London "Feltham" style cabs but retaining its open top. The rebuilding went well and the car was put back into service in August. It was painted in the striking red and cream livery of the "Feltham" cars and it looks just like a "Feltham" car, had one been made into an open top tram. Indeed many of the older visitors from London are fooled into thinking that it is one of the original trams that ran in the city! The destinations "North Finchley via Finsbury Park" and "Tottenham Court Road" enhance the London atmosphere of the tramcar.

May also saw the start of the extensions to the shop and tea rooms at Colyton. The major work was scheduled for the winter of 2000/01, so that visitors during the

**In its third incarnation car 12 shows its Feltham style ends and London livery.** *Seaton Tramway collection.*

**A very rare event. Car 12 meets with car 14 at Riverside curve, on the token controlled section of line. This was a special move and performed under direct supervision of the Operations Manager.** *Photograph authors.*

**The new entrance to Colyton terminus.** *Photograph authors.*

**The body of car 9 arriving at Seaton.** *Photograph Arthur Whitehouse.*

### Three New Trams

In 1986, before starting on the building of tramcar number 17, Allan had set out a rough design for a new type of tramcar, based on number 8. It was intended to build three new trams for the system. Working with Eric Thornton the design evolved. They took aspects from Blackburn tramcars, particularly the angled ends, though there are also elements of Plymouth and Brighton. The size was based broadly on number 12. So the design had a tramcar 32 feet long, 6 inches longer than number 12; the width was increased by a couple inches to five feet; while the height is the same and it would seat 56 people. Over the years the design was modified. For example the centre of the lower saloon was dropped to allow easy access for wheelchairs and other disabled people. Unlike the other trams the new ones would have four motors and air operated hydraulic disc brakes.

Steps were being taken to start manufacturing the new trams when Derek Shepherd paid the tramway a visit. Derek had set up Bolton Trams Limited, a company that initially restored (actually rebuilt) Bolton number 66 in 1981 that runs in Blackpool. Following that success his company had been contracted by Blackpool Tramways to rebuild OMO car 7 into a replica of the Vanguard Class. This was completed in 1987. So they were in a position to build more trams. When Allan mentioned the proposal to build three new tramcars Derek asked if Bolton Trams Limited could put in a quote. Seaton Tramway management seriously considered the idea of having

2000 season would not be affected and the facilities would be ready by March and the 2001 season. The builders moved on to the site in October and started removing old walls and demolishing the old toilets. This was in readiness to extend the shop and tea room, as well as building a new store. At the Seaton terminus a wheelchair ramp was added to make it easier and quicker to put wheelchairs on to number 17.

Meanwhile the Lisbon tram moved away. Number 730 was taken to a new home in East Anglia by its owner, Roger Harvey. The Tramway also featured on the BBC "Holiday Programme" broadcast during the winter 2000/01. The winter also saw the usual programme of maintenance work to keep the tramway in tip-top condition. The high priority items were the renewal of the overhead wire from Riverside Depot to Seaton Terminus. The wire suffers from the salt air and after a while the deterioration affects the power supply, causing a greater voltage drop along the line. The never ending job of pole painting would continue and trams 16 and 17 were identified for repainting, while retaining their liveries.

The October 2000 issue of "The Tramway Tribune" recorded what must be an all-time record. According to the publication tramcars numbers 2 and 17 were to have their controllers overhauled for the first time since 1898! How many appliances can be said to have a similar record of service.

**The wheel chair platform at Colyton, which makes loading car 17 much easier for everyone.** *Photograph authors.*

**Car 9 is craned into the back of the depot.** *Photograph Arthur Whitehouse.*

the new tramcars built outside the Modern Electric Tramways workshops. This would be a new venture, as every tram up to date had been completely built in-house. But it was becoming increasingly evident that the company staff had an increasing volume of maintenance to do. It was agreed that the building of the bodies would be contracted out, while the workshop would complete the mechanical and electrical engineering aspects. The contract was signed in October 2001 for Bolton Trams Limited to build the bodies of numbers 9, 10 and 11 to the specification laid down by Modern Electric Tramways. These were to become the first trams built for Claude Lane's tramway that were not constructed by the company.

## The Foot and Mouth Outbreak

The year 2001 saw the devastating Foot and Mouth outbreak which stopped all farm animal movement and the virtual shutting down of vast areas of the countryside. The 2001 season for the tramway started on 7th April, in the middle of the crisis. The tramway managers were very apprehensive and nervous. The newspapers were full of the

**The new bogies for cars 9, 10 and 11 are lined up in the workshop.** *Photograph authors.*

**Car 10 arrives in a similar way.** *Photograph Arthur Whitehouse.*

**Work starts on cars 9 and 10.** *Photograph authors.*

effect the crisis was having on the tourist market and the tramway was about to start its daily service. The South and East Devon areas were not directly affected, the nearest outbreaks being in North and West Devon, though East Devon did get into the headlines with the famous case of Phoenix the calf at Membury. However, the media were equally pessimistic for the tourist industry over the whole country. The tramway had made a significant investment in developing Colyton and it looked as if it could be a quiet year.

As it was, many coastal areas saw an increase in trade as people abandoned areas like Dartmoor for the more built-up resorts. To the relief of the tramway there was actually an increase in passengers. Easter proved a particularly busy time, being 30% busier than the year before, which itself was a record for the tramway. The extra facilities at Colyton proved themselves able to cope with the additional passengers. The wider range of souvenirs proved popular, increasing sales even further. An additional car was stationed at Seaton Terminus, allowing a full tram to leave soon after the arrival from Colyton.

The Tram Stop Restaurant at Colyton terminus proved a great success, with special events including jazz bands and theme evenings. East Devon District Council had taken over two tracts of land to the west of the tramway. One section called Colyford Common is north of Swan's Nest loop. The other is between the line and the River Axe going from the Riverside loop and Axmouth loop. These were designated as nature reserves. The local authority expressed interest in working with the tramway and are very keen on the bird watching specials, allowing enthusiasts to get a close view of the wild life. So the year saw a return of the bird watching trips and these proved very popular. The trips operate before and after normal running, so the tram is able to make frequent stops, the trip lasting around two hours. The number on each trip is restricted to 20 to enable tripods to be used for long telephoto shots. The tram operates as a mobile hide, giving minimum disturbance to the birds and other wild life. With an expert giving a commentary the trips are suitable for the novice as well as the expert and up to 45 different species can be seen during the trip.

For the year 2001 the tramway carried close to 92,000 passengers. A fine result in an uncertain year.

## Horses at Colyton

Before the 2001 season Sylvia Voysey, from Colyton, approached the company to ask if she could use the station approach to run a horse drawn wagon to take people to and from Colyton town centre. The tramway readily agreed. The venture got off to a late start owing to the Foot and Mouth restrictions. But once going it proved to be a popular added attraction and the "Wagon Wanderer" was a regular feature to be seen at Colyton. Two Suffolk Punch horses, Winston and Senator, drew the wagon, built by Mike Rowland a local wheelwright. The success was such that another cart was built for the 2002 season and now both wagons operate in the high season. The second cart being driven by Sylvia's son Richard.

## Number 6 Visits Camborne

In 1902 the only electric tramway to operate in Cornwall opened to provide a passenger and goods service between Camborne and Redruth. Historical and tramway enthusiasts felt that such an occasion should be remembered and so a Centenary Committee was established under the chairmanship of Colin Saxton. The centenary was held on 8th November, a Friday, with events taking place over the weekend. Colin Saxton contacted Seaton Tramway and asked if they could loan a tramcar for the event, since Seaton is the only operating tramway in the West Country. The well-travelled car 6 was selected and taken to Camborne on the back of a low loader with Mark Horner in attendance. During the celebrations it was displayed at Camborne, Redruth town centre and on the site of the old depot at Carn Brea, Pool, now a Safeways supermarket. On all these occasions it was joined by another tramcar, Peter Hallam's St Austell and District Tramways car 41, a miniature passenger carrying tram with portable track. This gave rides to children at the three venues and was very reminiscent of the early Claude Lane days when he took car 23 to fêtes.

The celebrations were formally opened by the Mayor of Camborne and though the weather was far from ideal it did not dampen the enthusiasm of the public from joining in with the events. The Seaton tramway gained useful publicity from the occasion.

## Allan Gardner Retires

Having celebrated his 65th birthday in 2002 Allan Gardner retired as Managing Director. This was no sudden decision, it had been planned for several years and the Tramway Company had been making the necessary preparations to ensure a smooth transition. Indeed this was very necessary as Allan had been at the helm for 31 years. He had taken on the rôle after the untimely death of Claude Lane and was just the second Managing Director in over 50 years of tramway running. This must be a record in the annals of tramway undertakings. Most tramways did not even last 50 years, let alone have such stable management.

The previous year it had been decided by the Board of Directors that Mark Horner would take up the Managing Director rôle, moving from his Operations and Marketing Director post. As Allan was also the Chief Engineer, this left a vacancy and James Hammett, the Electrical Engineer, became Chief Engineer. All were long standing employees of the tramway and the moves made a smooth transition. Allan himself continues to serve as a Director of the company and moved to work part time on engineering projects.

So on 1st May 2002 Allan Gardner retired as Managing Director. Allan did not want a great fuss, so the day itself was low key. But such an event could not take place without some recognition. Many old friends of Allan and the tramway turned up to wish him well for the future and to present gifts to mark the occasion. The event was particularly opportune as the first of the new trams, built by Bolton Trams Ltd, arrived at the tramway a couple of weeks earlier on 11th April. So Allan was able to see the arrival of the new era of trams that he had planned.

**Allan Gardner at work in the Company Board Room.** *Photograph authors.*

But of course it would be impossible to keep Allan away from the tramway and he is now to be seen three days a week helping with engineering and other work of the tramway.

## The New Trams Arrive

Number 9 was delivered to Seaton on 11th April 2002. The body arrived on a low loader and was placed on temporary caster wheels and pushed into the paint shop. Here it received a livery of mid blue, light blue and white. It was very reminiscent of the experimental livery used by Glasgow on its experimental one way car number 1005. Cars 10 and 11 were delivered on the 7th and 13th August respectively. Number 10 has a standard Glasgow livery of orange, green and ivory, while number 11 was given a livery based on the Liverpool First Class tramcars of 1909, with white and cream. The lettering, numbers and fancy scrollwork were provided by Stan Letts, although this was not without incident, when part of the lettering on number 9 had to be removed and remade, as some of it had been put in the wrong place.

The year 2003 sees the Golden Jubilee of Modern Electric Tramways. The small trams were started by Claude Lane when number 23 rolled out of the Barnet workshops in 1949, some 54 years ago. But it was not until the Eastbourne operation in 1953 that Modern Electric Tramways was set up as a company, which has been the parent company for Eastbourne Tramways and for Seaton and District Tramway.

## Mark Horner

Mark has been managing the tramway for a year and has continued to build on the very firm foundations set by Claude Lane and Allan Gardner. He was pleased to see that the tramway performed very well in 2002, setting new records for passengers.

So the 50th anniversary sees a new Managing Director. It started with some very welcome news. In the Excellence in England Awards the tramway was named as the Small Visitor Attraction of the year 2002/2003 for the South West of the UK. It goes forward to the National Ceremony later in the year.

At the time of writing the new trams are still under construction and the hope is that at least one can be rolled out for test running as part of the Golden Jubilee celebrations.

**Mark Horner driving car 4.** *Seaton Tramway collection.*

# CHAPTER 7

# How to Run a Tramway

This is an opportunity to tell you what happens behind the scenes to ensure that the tramway runs smoothly and safely for all passengers. Safety is the first concern of the tramway and everything is done to protect the well being of all passengers and staff. In the 54 years that the trams have been operating there has been no accident resulting in any serious injury to any passenger or member of the public.

When it is recalled that in the very early days at the fêtes the trams were often driven by children, with just a smattering of training, it is a superb record. These days the tramway is a professional operation and it takes a far more serious approach. In common with all British tramways all the drivers are trained in house by the tramway. They are all required to pass a test before they are allowed to drive in service. Another major difference from the early days is that anyone under the age of 21 is not permitted to be a driver.

**A young driver at Eastbourne, something never seen at Seaton.** *Photograph Ron Howes.*

## A Typical Day

The usual routine day starts before opening the tramway when the Duty Traffic Supervisor checks the weather forecast for the day, to get a rough idea of what the demand for tram rides will be. Staff arriving at the depot check whether there are any specials during the day and if visitors have pre-booked a wheelchair ride on number 17. Meanwhile the shop staff at Seaton and Colyton termini open up and prepare to sell the first tickets of the day. The depot doors are opened and the first tram leaves, heading for Seaton.

During the summer, the normal service requires three trams, leaving Seaton terminus at twenty minute intervals. The departure times from Seaton and Colyton allow the trams to pass each other at Axmouth loop and Tye Lane loop. All the points and overhead frogs on the loops are sprung to automatically direct the trams to the left, except for the Riverside loop where the trams take the right hand road. This is due to the track layout required to have access to the depot.

The tramway has found it can give a better service to the public by running the service with four tramcars. This allows the Seaton terminus always to have a tramcar for people to board. So intending passengers see their tram and they are not left in a queue with no tram in sight. Therefore most days see four trams in service. Visitors boarding at the Seaton end find that there is always a tramcar available. So when the tram from Colyton arrives a loaded tram is ready to leave, ensuring that the service keeps to its timetable. This also means there is no pressure on the passengers of the arriving tram to alight quickly. They can leave at their leisure and the tram is ready to take on passengers until the time comes for it to leave for Colyton.

**A busy day at Seaton, with queues waiting for the next tram.** *Photograph John H Meredith.*

To run this level of service five drivers are required each day. But as the tramway operates seven days a week and drivers need to have rest days off, a total of 13 drivers on rotating shifts are required. This enables all drivers to have at least two days off each week. On top of this there are the inevitable bouts of sickness when additional drivers need to be brought in quickly. To help with this and for the special event days, there is a policy where all members of staff who are eligible, that is between 21 years old and 70 years old, are qualified drivers. So if something happens and someone is needed to drive at very short notice, there are several people who can step into the breach.

**A reminder to every driver before entering the token controlled section of track.** *Photograph authors.*

Most of the tramway operates on what is called 'line of sight'. This is exactly like driving a car. The driver does not have any signals, but drives with a clear view of the track ahead and knows that he/she must wait at the appropriate loop for the approaching tram to pass. There are two places where this arrangement does not happen. The first is the track from Seaton Terminus to Riverside Depot. This section has some very tight turns that are obscured by trees. So the driver cannot get a clear view of the track well ahead. So to prevent any chance of two trams meeting head to head the section is protected by a staff system. There is a special piece of wood (it was originally a leg on one of Claude's chairs!) with a large metal loop on it, called a staff, which normally has to be carried by the tram entering the section. The staff carries a brass plate engraved with "Riverside to Seaton Staff". So this means that only one tram can be on that part of the line at any one time. The first tram of the day picks up the staff and takes it to Seaton Terminus. It then brings it back to Riverside on its first passenger journey. At the Riverside loop there is a special hook that the driver puts the staff on to. This allows the tram from Colyton to

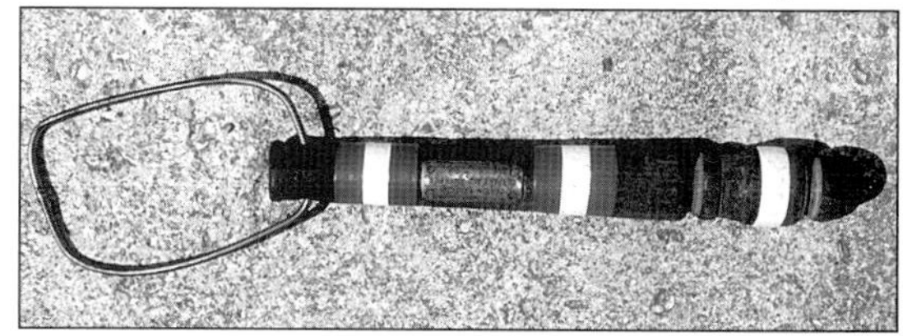

**Once a leg on Claude's chair and now the token for the Riverside to Seaton terminus section.** *Photograph authors.*

**The driver of 7 stops during his journey to Colyton to leave the staff on the special hook at the Riverside loop.** *Photograph authors.*

**Colyford in its final form.** *Photograph authors.*

pick up the staff before entering the protected section of track.

The other place where the 'line of sight' does not apply is at the level crossing at Colyford. This is the one place on the line where the trams come across road traffic. To ensure safety, traffic lights have been fitted at the crossing. When a tram needs to cross the road the driver will drive up to the crossing and press a plunger to switch on the crossing lights. A white light starts to flash in the direction of the tram, indicating to the driver that the red lights are working on the road and that the tram can proceed. The road traffic is halted by the flashing red lights, like many railway level crossings. Keeping an eye open for the road traffic the tram crosses the road. This can produce some entertainment for the drivers as occasionally tourists in the area, who are unaware of the tramway, are amazed to see a tramcar crossing the road in front of them. Once clear of the crossing the tram runs over a track-mounted treadle to automatically de-activate the lights and allow the road traffic to proceed.

Many groups visiting the tramway will pre-book a tram just for their party, that runs as an extra car. The tramway always ensures that the tram is available a few minutes before the appointed time. However, many of these trips are booked by coach companies, and given the difficulties of the roads, they are sometimes a little later than booked. So everything has to be flexible to make sure that the extra car is ready. So it is placed on the spur siding out of the way of the service cars. Now you may be thinking how does the tramway run if the extra car has the staff? No other tram can enter the protected section from Riverside to Seaton. But there are arrangements that allow this to happen. The extra car will travel either in tandem with or six minutes behind a service car. The first tram is shown the staff, but does not pick it up. The second, extra tram, then takes the staff to Seaton, knowing that there is another tram in front. The extra car then has to wait at Seaton until it can travel back to Riverside with another service tram, using the same arrangements.

The extra cars are sometimes used by coach companies as part of a round trip. The coach drops off the group at Seaton, they travel on the tram and the coach picks them up again at Colyton. Other specials do the return trip with their group, with a short or long break at Colyton.

For additional safety all the drivers of the service trams are informed when the special is running, when it leaves the terminus and in which loops it will pass the service cars. This sounds very complicated, but in fact the passengers do not notice anything – it all works smoothly. All the drivers have two way radios and are in contact with the Traffic Supervisor, who co-ordinates the service and keeps drivers informed of any additional cars on the line. It also means that the drivers can get in contact with the Traffic Supervisor to report any problems or delays.

The tramway can often cater for disabled visitors at short notice. Number 17, the wheelchair tramcar, is held in readiness for such occasions. The driver removes the necessary seats to allow the wheelchair(s) and their attendants to ride on the tram. When number 17 was first built it was necessary to place a portable

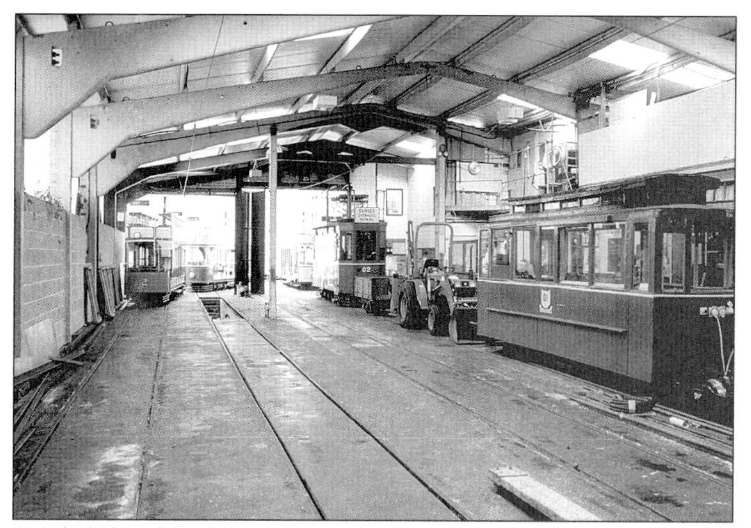

**A typical view of the depot during a busy running day. The only vehicles are the maintenance cars. 02 is kept at the entrance to the depot, ready to go out to deal with any emergency.** *Photograph authors.*

**02 and the drop side trailer. The wheel barrow indicates work to be done.** *Photograph authors.*

**One of the new bogies for 9, 10 and 11, something that the maintenance engineers need to be familiar with.** *Photograph authors.*

ramp against the tramcar and push the wheelchairs up at a steep angle. But now permanent brick platforms have been built at both Seaton and Colyton to make access quick and easy, which means that car 17 can now be operated as a normal timetabled car even if it has to carry people in their wheelchairs.

All day an eye is kept on the numbers of people wanting to ride the trams. If there is a sudden influx extra trams can be added. The driver shift system allows for a standby driver to take on extras as required. These run in addition to the normal service trams, so the timetable is kept, with the extras running between the trams on the advertised timetable.

During the peak summer holidays in July and August the tramway operates a six car service. This is achieved by adding a tram behind each normal service car. These extra cars run six minutes behind each service car. For example a service car will leave Seaton terminus and head for Axmouth loop where it passes the incoming service car. Six minutes later the extra car leaves Seaton Terminus and so passes the incoming service car at Riverside loop. Basically an extra car runs a loop behind each of the three service cars.

Operation continues, with the standby driver taking on the trams around midday to allow the other drivers to take their well earned lunch breaks. The time of the last tram varies according to the month. For most of the year the last tram leaves Colyton for Seaton at 5.30pm (BST) or 4.30pm (GMT), but during the summer peak period the last tram leaves Colyton for Seaton at 9.10pm. After the last tram the shops and Tram Stop Restaurant are closed and tidied and cleaned ready for the next day.

## Behind the Scenes

In addition to the staff the public meet driving the trams and running the shops, there are the most important maintenance staff. During the summer maintenance is kept to routine work. Exceptionally they will tackle some larger projects on individual tramcars, but this is rare. Regular maintenance is carried out on the track and overhead to ensure it is kept in good working order. Major work, such as replacement of overhead or track, is left to the winter months, when the maintenance gang can have full access to the track and overhead.

Of course there are sometimes unexpected problems that have to be sorted out. Like all tramways using trolley poles there are odd occasions when a trolley pole will become de-wired, no matter how careful the drivers are. The trolley poles have been designed to minimise any damage to the overhead should they de-wire. The trolley head is detachable and if the pole is de-wired the head will slip off before it can pull down overhead wires. The head is stopped from falling to the ground by a safety wire or chain. But it does mean that the maintenance gang have to quickly travel out to the tram and either repair it immediately or tow it back to the depot.

**Working on the overhead in the very early days. But the techniques used have not changed since then.** *Seaton Tramway collection.*

After an occurrence such as this and before the engineers leave, the overhead is inspected to make sure that it is not damaged and to see what it was that caused the dewiring. If it was a fault on the overhead this has to be repaired immediately. Works car 02 is taken out and the repairs are done while the service cars still operate. All the drivers are told of the nature and location of the problem and proceed through it under the engineer's supervision.

People are often surprised that the engineers can work on the overhead while the trams are running. After all there are 120 volts running through the overhead wire. The reason is the same one that lets birds sit on high voltage cables without any harm. Provided whoever, or whatever, touches the live wire does not complete an electrical circuit by touching the rails, all is well. The tramway told us that this was the reason that they had a policy of not employing anyone over 16 feet tall (the height of the overhead wire)! On the tramway the engineers have to be lifted to the overhead wire. To do this they use the tower platform on works car 02 or the hydraulic hoist wagon, affectionately known as "The Bucket".

**02 during its days as a trailer, behind the Ruston diesel.** *Seaton Tramway collection.*

## Technicalities

The trams all have two motors each of which is wired through the controller at each end (the new trams have four motors, which are paired and otherwise wired the same). The driver has a special 'key' that fits on to the controller and without it the tram cannot operate. It is rather like the ignition key on a car, except the tram does not need a starter! The tram driver has fewer controls to worry about than a car driver. The first thing that a tram does not need is a steering wheel. The rails take care of that. So the driver has the controller, operated by the left hand and the handbrake operated by the right hand. The controller not only puts power into the motors, it also has an electrical braking capability. The hand brake is used to pull up slowly and hold the tram stationary. The brakes operate on all the

**Purchased with the track bed, the Southern railway concrete platelayers hut at Colyford is now used as a generator station.** *Photograph authors.*

wheels. In addition there is a foot pedal that operates the warning gong or whistle. Cars 4, 9, 10, 11, 12 and 17 also have air brakes in addition to the handbrakes.

But these are not the only things that the driver has to be aware of. There is a breaker switch, which is fitted between the power coming from the trolley pole and the controller. This is like your fuse box at home. If anything happens that causes an excess current the breaker switch will trip out and stop power to the motors. This ensures that the motors and other sensitive equipment are not harmed by too much power. The switch can be tripped by an over zealous driver trying to accelerate too quickly. There is also a light bulb in the cab, called a "line light", that tells the driver that he has power from the overhead. As an additional aid there is also a buzzer that operates when there is a sudden change of supply current. It gives a short buzz when the trolley head passes across a frog and a long buzz when there is a major break in the supply, such as a trolley coming off the overhead. In such a case drivers must make an emergency stop, to prevent damage to the overhead by a stray trolley. Trainee drivers are tested by giving an emergency brake command and they must stop the tramcar within the distance between two overhead traction poles.

The electrical supply is taken from the mains at Seaton, Colyford and Colyton. The mains AC voltage is transformed to 120 volts DC which in turn charges battery sets at each generating point. An additional, battery-only feed point is located near Axmouth Loop, which is kept up to the correct voltage by means of a trickle charge from Riverside and Colyford.

## Special Days

Several times through the year the tramway has special

**Sometimes the drivers volunteer beyond the normal call of duty. During the Teddy Bear's Picnic day the driver of 6 wears a full teddy bear costume.** *Seaton Tramway collection.*

events. There is the annual Bus and Vintage Vehicle Rally, when the tramway is host to many historic vehicles, that are displayed for the public to view. There are also Gala days and the tramway takes part in the Seaton and Colyton Carnivals. During the carnivals the tramway runs late into the night and for both occasions the takings for the day are donated to the carnival charity.

On these special days and particularly during the vehicle rally, an intensive timetable is run. The most hectic time is when a nine car service is run. To pack this number of trams on the line requires careful planning and making sure that all the drivers know exactly where they are meant to be in relation to the other trams. We were shown the timetable that the drivers work to on these busy days and it looks like a puzzle set by Mensa to determine who can join their society! In this scheme two trams leave Seaton terminus, the usual service car with an extra behind it. Six minutes later the second extra leaves the terminus. The service car goes to Axmouth loop, while its partner extra stays at Riverside loop. The second extra then goes to Riverside to join the preceding extra. When the incoming service car has passed the two extra cars work as a pair up the line to Colyton, six minutes behind their service car. Working the reverse direction the trams leave Colyton at six minute intervals (or one loop apart). At Riverside loop an occasional tramcar has to wait and work the staff controlled section as a pair. We suggest if you really want to discover how this all works you must visit the tramway during the vehicle rally.

## The Tram Driving Experience

One very popular feature of the tramway is the Tram Driving Experience. Pre-booking is advisable, though occasionally last minute arrangements can be made. The aspiring Motormen have either a half day or a full day tram driving. A special car is allocated and the trainee tram drivers arrive ready for their day ahead. They are given a guided tour of the depot. Under expert supervision they are given lessons on how the tram operates and all the important safety information. Then they get to drive the tram themselves. The tram is treated as a 'special' and fits in around the normal service cars. On the half day course the driver drives for one full round trip (six miles lasting an hour). The full day course gives the opportunity for three full round trips and two short workings, a total of 24 miles of tram driving. The day includes morning tea or coffee, lunch and an afternoon cream tea, all at the Tram Stop Restaurant at Colyton. This is a unique hands-on experience and many a lucky husband has been given a surprise birthday present that they will never forget. The tramway has even gained new volunteers from these days.

## Bird Watching Trips

On his first visit to Seaton, Claude Lane saw a diesel unit running along the river and was captivated by the beauty of the scene. He realised that if he could purchase the line and build his tramway the sylvan atmosphere would also attract future visitors. In fact the tramway runs alongside two beautiful nature reserves, Seaton Marshes and Colyford Common. Right from the start it was realised that the line offered amazing opportunities to see wild birds and other fauna. Indeed the more bird inclined tram builders would see how many different species they could spot. By the time the first trams ran to Bobsworth Bridge they realised that the tramway was unique in giving an opportunity to see many birds that would never normally be seen. The early guide books for the line announced that as many as 53 different varieties of British birds had been observed in a single day from the trams.

At an early stage several bird watching societies contacted the tramway to enquire if they could go on special bird watching trips by tram. This led to the idea of having Guided Bird Watching Trips on a regular basis. To ensure that the normal tram service did not interfere with the bird watching or visa versa the trips are run out of normal hours. There is a break during the busy summer months, when the number of species to be seen is at its lowest.

On each trip there is an expert ornithologist who provides a commentary on the birds that can be seen. The tram becomes a mobile hide and the birds are very used to seeing them running up and down the line and know that they never offer any threat. It is only when the passengers get out that the birds become disturbed. But it is necessary to move from the tram to walk to the permanent hide at the base of a flood bank. Here an even closer view can be had of marshland birds.

The trip is limited to 20 persons so that everyone can get a good view and there is space for those with cameras and tripods. In addition to the birds that can be seen there are also other forms of wild life. Foxes and Roe Deer are often seen. A less common sighting is of badgers. The trips take around two hours and are an excellent way of seeing some of the less common wild life of the country.

## Santa Specials

For many years the tramway has been celebrating Christmas with a series of Santa Specials on the weekends immediately before Christmas Day. The event starts at Seaton Terminus with a tram journey to Colyton in one of the enclosed tramcars. Here seasonal refreshments are served and the children can see Santa in his Grotto and get a present. This is a wonderful way to start the Christmas celebrations.

## Television Interest

The tramway has had plenty of interest from television companies. Generally the interest comes from either children's programmes or from holiday programmes. The former have proved to be remarkably helpful in raising interest and visitors in the tramway. What the tramway did not expect was that the programmes have had a regular series of repeats, bringing the tramway to

**At Colyford the only part of the original station that survives is the Victorian Gents toilet.** *Photograph authors.*

a new audience each time. Whenever the repeats are shown the tramway knows about it because they get lots of phone calls making enquiries about making a visit. Holiday programmes tend to get less repeats, but the initial showing always brings new interest.

The other way that television can help the tramway is when there are very special events. The local station was very interested when number 14 was launched by Larry Grayson. They were also present when the Mayor of Exeter formally launched rebuilt Exeter car 19.

## Winter Work

Major track and overhead work is scheduled for the winter, when the track gang can have the tramway to themselves. But winter, even in East Devon, can be cold and bitter. So number 01 has been fitted out as a ganger's trailer. It goes out behind number 02 and acts as a shelter and respite for the nastier days. Windy Corner was named by the first gang that laid track to the Seaton terminus and no one has felt it necessary to change the name. On a cold winters day the ganger's trailer becomes a most attractive place. It also doubles as a mobile mess room for tea and lunch breaks. It even has a sink fitted on the platform at one end.

The type of work carried out is renewal of overhead or track. Relaying parts of the track that need to be renewed, or eased, or where requirements change. Obviously removing a section of track would be extremely disruptive during the summer operation, but in the winter there is no such problem, though work has to be well planned to ensure that the Christmas Santa specials are free to run.

# CHAPTER 8

# The Future of the Seaton Tramway

With cars 9, 10 and 11 the fleet has been increased by 30%. This gives additional, more easily accessible seating for visitors. However the management of the tramway still have some ideas for extending the fleet. The tramway would like to build another tramcar (car 20) for hot summer days based on the Llandudno and Colwyn Bay Toastrack tramcars. These are completely open tramcars. Basically they consist of a flat floor with a series of cross bench seats. This harks back very much to the original number 6, built for operation at Voryd Park, but rejected by the Twigdons. If built it is likely to be a very popular car with visitors. Certainly when the

**11 and 9 in the workshop being fitted with their electrical equipment.** *Photograph authors.*

**9 and 10 painted, lined and lettered. The electrical work is being completed and then the upper deck seats will be fitted.** *Photograph authors.*

**9 and 10 being fitted out. 10 has had its bogies fitted, while the bogie of 9 is standing on the track in front of the tram.** *Photograph authors.*

National Tramway Museum at Crich ran their Blackpool Toastrack number 167 it was always in great demand. What could be nicer than riding on an open tramcar on a sunny day along the line. Let us hope this proposal comes into being.

Visitors to the tramway may wonder what the framework is that can be seen on the siding at Colyford. It was used to enable some volunteer engineers to become proficient welders. There was a vague thought that it might become a crossbench trailer, number 27, for car 17. However, there are other options that are more likely.

Another favourite design of tramcar is the single deck 'room and kitchen' cars that ran in Glasgow. This could be a possible idea for a future tramcar. This car would be an enclosed single deck saloon, capable of taking wheelchairs from the existing ramps at Seaton and Colyton.

## Track Developments

One proposal that is very much in the forefront is placing a new loop at Leeds Bridge. This would move the single track staff section from Riverside loop to Leeds Bridge. Currently the section of single track using the staff dictates the frequency of the tram service. Adding the new loop will give a better balance to the operation. It will mean that all the loops will be roughly the same distance apart. For timetable purposes all the loops will be three minutes apart. On very busy days a six-minute service could be operated, requiring ten trams. With three extra trams soon entering service there will be a real opportunity to provide a more frequent service and the line will be able to carry more passengers.

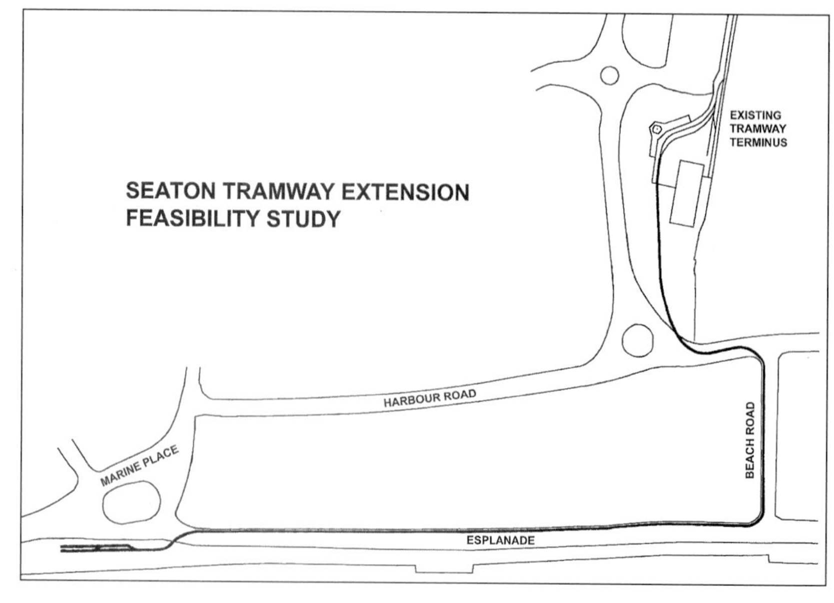

**Seaton Tramway would like to build a tramcar based on the Llandudno toastrack. 19 shows how attractive the tram will be to visitors on a sunny day.** *Photograph TLRS Archive.*

## Other Possibilities

The tramway would very much like to open a visitor centre and exhibition area. Here aspects of the tramway that visitors would otherwise not see, particularly the history of Claude Lane and his trams and an insight into the operation of the Seaton Tramway. Currently there is no suitable building for such a museum. But who knows what might happen in future.

## A Tramway to Seaton Town Centre?

In 1998 the Council approached the tramway company to inform them that it had been seriously debating the possibility of the company extending the tramway, as a street tramway, to reach the town centre. This would require a feasibility study and they needed to know what the reaction of the company was before committing to the study. The Company was very keen and would fully assist in any study. The Council appointed Ross Silcock in June 1998 to undertake an initial study. The study examined the technical, legal and economic aspects of the proposals. The report was completed in May 1999 and the conclusions were that there were significant financial benefits for the town. Two possible tram routes were identified and put out for public comment. The public were in support and preferred the esplanade route. The consultants emphasised that for the full benefit to be gained there must be co-ordination between the tramway extension and the council's improvements to the sea front.

Ross Silcock were commissioned again in 2000 to report on detailed proposals to extend the tramway on street from its current terminus to a point near Marine Place. The aim was to have a report that would be used to secure the necessary legislative authority and undertake the work. The proposed route would leave the existing terminus, turn left onto Harbour Road (the B3172), then turn right into Beach Road. At the end of Beach Road it would turn right and run along the Esplanade to the large island in Marine Place. Here a new terminus would be built. Apart from the new terminus and the short section to Harbour Road, the new route would be all road running. However, wherever possible, the tram line would be clearly distinguished from the normal road and raised to prevent road traffic from using it and pedestrians would also be discouraged from walking in the track.

The overhead wire would need to be 5.8m high and a new sub-station would be required. It is likely that the existing tramcars would not be able to be used and some new vehicles would be needed. The reasons for these changes to that used on the existing tramway is that, while the tramway was built under a Light Railway Order, it is in law defined as a "Tramroad" while the extension is a "Street Tramway". The difference being that a tramroad is constructed off the highway while a street tramway is constructed within a highway. Thus a tramroad does not have any interaction with other vehicles or pedestrians. So Street Tramways have many more regulations.

So will the tramway extend to the town's streets? Well unfortunately the proposals are looking less likely. First the finances required are substantial. The estimate is in excess of £600,000. However, further discussion with Her Majesty's Railways Approvals

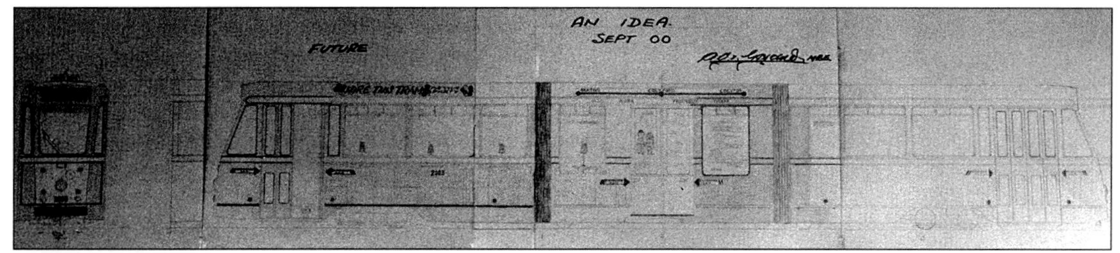

**A glimpse of the future? A drawing of a single deck articulated tramcar with distinct Brussels influence.** *Photograph authors.*

Inspectorate (HMRI) indicates that the new tramcars required will need to be similar to the new generation of light rail vehicles, such as those at Croydon and Sheffield. Apart from the cost, this will remove the traditional aspect of the tramway that tourists like. Indeed it is the open top nature of the tramcars that is the major attraction. The HMRI have already stated that open top tramcars will not be acceptable on the street running section.

But while in the management offices at Seaton we saw pinned to the wall a preliminary drawing by Allan Gardner of a single deck articulated tramcar with Brussels influence. This is the type of tram that could possibly be operated over such an extension. So is this the future for the tramway?

## Final Thoughts

The tramway is a great believer in having fun, not only for its passengers, but also for the volunteers and staff. An example can be found in the workshop toilets. A box is positioned above the cistern with the following notice. "The cost of this toilet seat was £30.00. Please acknowledge the generosity of the management in providing it by donating one penny in the box each time use is made of it."

It is very clear that the tramway came into being because of the dreams of one man, Claude Lane. Others, particularly Allan Gardner, picked up those dreams and made them real. In turn they have dreams of what can become of the tramway. The visitor centre and the new trams already mentioned are some of the dreams. Whether it will be possible to realise all these wishes is uncertain. But what is very clear is that the Seaton Tramway will not stay still. It will continue to develop and give immense pleasure to the thousands of visitors riding on the trams each year.

Claude ran his first tram in 1949. The company he established, Modern Electric Tramways Limited, has completed its first fifty years. This is longer than many town tramways lasted! After fifty years the company and the tramway is in better shape than it has ever been. Winner of many prestigious awards for tourism it continues to attract more visitors and is set for another superb fifty years giving pleasure to all its visitors.

# APPENDIX 1

# Monograms (and other Decalcomania) by Stan Letts

Although I had sampled the trams at Eastbourne in 1958, it was to be another seventeen years before I became reacquainted with them in their new Seaton home. In the meantime, in the mid-'60s, I had become involved in the first bus preservation project in my native West Midlands. This involvement was to have a profound effect, with significant implications for the Seaton Tramway.

**Stan Letts applying varnish to the back of the transfer in readiness to pressing it on to the tram body, or in this case to wooden plaques that will be screwed to the tramcar.** *Photograph authors.*

**After allowing the varnish to dry the transfer paper is removed by soaking with water.** *Photograph authors.*

The restoration of our pre-war Birmingham Corporation Daimler involved returning it to its original livery (which had been cheapened in post-war years), and we were faced with the impossible task of finding transfers of the original ornate fleet numbers and other lettering. They therefore had to be re-created by hand and to my own surprise I found that I could make a fair fist of the job (despite being dismissed as a no-hoper by the Arts Master back in my schooldays). By experimentation we found also that we could re-create the principles of making our own varnish-fixing transfers. Here things have to be done backwards, which is to say that everything has to be done "mirror-image", and one starts with the coat of varnish and finishes up with the undercoat. All painting has to be done on a water-soluble gummed surface, and for our embryonic attempts we found that using ordinary gummed labels achieved the desired results.

In the mid- to late-1970s a very good friend had retired to live in Lyme Regis, just a few miles away from Seaton, and he was a generous host to some enjoyable summer holidays. Being a tram enthusiast himself he had already made the acquaintance of Allan Gardner, so it was inevitable that I should be introduced. I was naturally intrigued to see the trams at close quarters in Riverside Depot, but couldn't help noticing that all the lettering, etc., was obviously (but superbly) hand-painted. Allan told me that the "Modern Electric Tramways" monogram on the cars had been devised and painted by him, dating back to their time at Eastbourne. I suggested to Allan that now the company was trading as the Seaton & District Electric Tramway, a new monogram to this effect might be more appropriate, especially as the Tramway was openly promoting a "vintage" and very much non-modern, image, this being clearly what attracted visitors. He agreed, but was understandably averse to scrapping his original design, and we compromised by his agreeing to my going away to devise something suitable, which could be displayed on the trams in addition to the M.E.T. original.

I already had in my mind's eye the ornate oval monogram, containing intertwined letters, that had graced the buses of my employers (Midland Red). I was puzzling how to intertwine the letters "SDET" when by a happy chance a book on the Tramways of North East England by my good friend George Hearse showed me how. It contained a reproduction of the monogram of the Sunderland District Electric Tramways, which incorporated the same intertwined initial letters of that company. I therefore made some transfers, which appeared in 1978.

Compared with those I subsequently developed, I will agree with any critic that this, my first attempt at an SDET monogram, was quite crude, and was very ill-matched when paired with Allan Gardner's original.

When "Boat" No. 4 was being restored to its green-and-cream livery after its "purple" spell celebrating the Queen's Silver Jubilee in 1977, the chance was taken of making a more professional-looking job of the SDET monogram. The woven "SDET" was all that remained of the original, while the garter was made round instead of oval. The plain edges were replaced by "gold braid". A more ornate "buckle" was sought, and I found just the thing in a book on old railway monograms. Most appropriately it was the buckle off the London & South Western Railway monogram, on whose trackbed the Seaton Tramway was now laid. The dominant colour of the garter would be red, as was the first attempt.

This gave the opportunity of creating a matching replacement for the original MET monogram. The same gold-braided round garter and LSWR buckle was used, but with the "Modern Electric Tramways Ltd" title round the garter. Inside the circle I devised a riband which contained wording celebrating Claude Lane as Founder. Out went the representation of a trolley-wheel (the Seaton trams all used carbon-slipper heads) to be replaced by a representation of a tram wheel. Not quite by co-incidence was the fact that I had just re-created the B.E.T. "Magnet & Wheel" monogram for the tram I was painting at the Black Country Museum at Dudley. The dominant colour of this garter was green, representing the "fleet" colour of the trams originated by Claude Lane.

These two monograms remained in use, two of each per car, for the next fifteen years or so. The only modification was to the SDET monogram, and this came about through a realisation that most of us had got something wrong. Around the garter read, "Seaton & District Electric Tramway Co.". It was the realisation that the SDET was not, of itself, a company. The company was (and is) Modern Electric Tramways Limited, and this company runs the tramway at Seaton. So the "Co." has now been omitted, not only from the

**The first monogram designed by Allan Gardner and used by the Modern Electric Tramways Company at Eastbourne and brought to Seaton.** *Photograph Stan Letts.*

**Stan Letts first transfer using the Seaton and District Electric Tramway title, a monogram with intertwined letters in an oval belt.** *Photograph Stan Letts.*

monogram, but also from all the titles displayed along the rocker panels of those cars which had hitherto been wrong. (This fact may be useful in dating a photograph – if the company title on the rocker panel is wrong, then the shot was taken before the late 1990s.)

By the 1990s the techniques for producing all my transfers had improved dramatically. The early ones were produced by having to trace, very laboriously, every scrap of black outline before any colouring could be applied. There was also the vexed question of making gold letters. Gold paint in the early days "went off" very quickly, and I actually used genuine gold-leaf in the earliest transfers. Now, improved technology had progressed to the point where all the laborious black outlines could be printed directly on to the transfer paper with a laser printer, and gold paint was now available which would never go off.

The "two of each per car" was used on the big single-decker 14. But it proved impractical on 16. This car had the "MET" monogram on one side of the tram, and the "SDET" one on the other. Allan Gardner and I chewed this one over at length, and we both came to the conclusion that two different monograms for the same organisation was a bit bizarre. However, to make one monogram out of the two risked compromising the Tramway's merchandising, where souvenirs, sweatshirts, ties, etc., all contained a representation of the SDET monogram.

To get over this problem, the SDET monogram was essentially retained, but room was made within the design to insert two ribands, one stating "Modern Electric Tramways Limited", and the other maintaining the wording celebrating the founding by Claude Lane. The ribands would be in green and cream perpetuating his original choice of those two colours. This combined design was accepted by the management and since then the trams have been given one monogram when repainted.

**How the two monograms were used on the Seaton tramcars.** *Photograph authors.*

However, another unpleasant prospect loomed. I was getting no younger, and the time was approaching when I would no longer be able to produce these transfers. I resolved to make a large bulk supply which, at the rate of two-per-tram, and an expected two trams repainted each year, would last the Tramway for some twenty years or more. By that time other printing technologies would have developed to the extent of being able to print any design, perhaps directly on to a tram. One never knows! So the design was put to a firm of transfer printers (who, incidentally, had invented the original varnish-fixing transfer in 1856, and they are still going strong in Birmingham). Despite being a most friendly firm who bent over backwards to do their best for me, the price was still prohibitive. So I set to do them myself, at home, giving thanks for the tremendous help now available from my home computer.

I had not done more than sixteen, when I realised just how tedious and soul-destroying was the fiddly and extremely time-consuming task of gold-infilling all the thirty letters round each garter. In my final design, intended for application to the new trams delivered in 2002, the letters are now black, with an additional dropped shading, which my laser-printer will print in a couple of seconds. Because the red background caused the black letters to show up poorly I have lightened it to a brighter vermilion, which has the advantage of not "disappearing" when applied to the side of a red tram (indeed it will show up against any

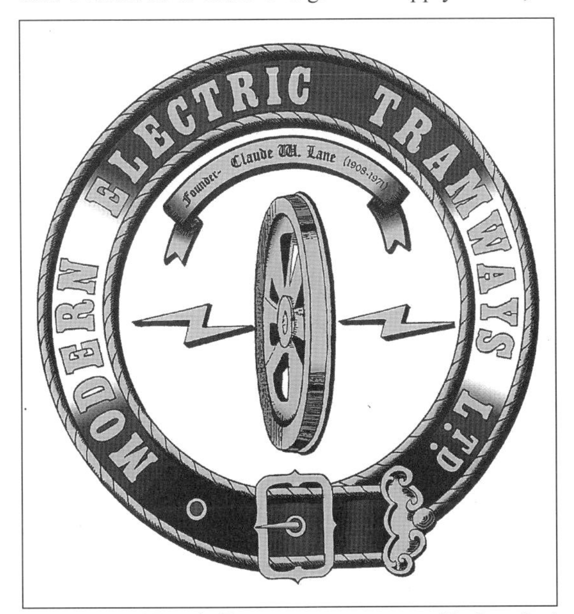


**The Modern Electric Tramways monogram with the wheel and lightning replacing the trolley wheel.**

**The same monogram on a tramcar, but with a more ornate buckle.** *Photograph Stan Letts.*

of the colours currently scheduled for the fleet). This final design, on which I am sure I cannot improve, is shown below.

As a postscript, I want to say that I have always been made most welcome at the Seaton Tramway, and everyone has been most forbearing in giving me a most remarkably free rein in designing, producing and applying most of the lettering and other ornamentation on most of the Seaton fleet. My "working holidays" at Seaton (often at the end of the winter when trams fresh out of the paintshop have to be finished ready for the start of the operating season) have been most enjoyable. Over nearly a quarter of a century, the Seaton Tramway has been the "proving-ground" for the development of my transfer-making capabilities. Without this experience I would not have been able to decorate the heritage trams at Birkenhead. It was my work on the Seaton trams which led me to being asked to do likewise on the restored Stockport 5, which led to my being asked to "do" Bolton 66, both now running on the Blackpool tramway. This in turn led to what is perhaps the final accolade, being asked by Blackpool Transport Services Ltd to make and apply all the interior and exterior transfers to their standard car 147 restored for the 2002 season. I therefore have cause to be very grateful to all at the Seaton Tramway.

**The latest monogram for Seaton and District Electric Tramways, incorporating the Modern Electric Tramways Company and Claude Lane as founder.** *Photograph Stan Letts.*

# APPENDIX 2

# The Tramcar Fleet

For most British tramway systems the numbering of tramcars is the most quirky part of the whole operation. The most bizarre example was the single tram comprising the whole of the Fintona horse tram fleet, which carried the number 381! Even the modern tramway systems have some oddities. Croydon Tramlink started its fleet with number 2530, which was the next number from the old London Transport trams fleet. In Sheffield the fleet starts with number 101. This is because the computer was set for three digit numbers and originally 001 was allocated to the first tram, but the management objected to numbers starting with zeros so it became 101.

At first glance, the Modern Electric Tramways fleet numbers seems very strange. However, a closer look shows that there is a logic behind the way that each tram was given a number.

It all started with 23. Now this tram is based on the two tramcars built by English Electric for the Darwen tramway system. These were numbered 23 and 24. Later they were sold to the Llandudno and Colwyn Bay Electric Railway. Here they retained their numbers, though due to a lack of clear communications the painter swapped the numbers on the trams. When Claude built his miniature replica he used the lower of the two numbers. So the first tram was given the number 23. In the records it was shown as number 1 in the fleet.

The next tram was another based on a prototype tramcar, this time one of the Boat designs at Blackpool. These trams originally carried the numbers 225 to 236. So Claude again chose the lowest number of the Class. In fact 225 was slightly different from the rest of the Class, but Claude probably did not spot that. This was the second tram to be built.

Then came the four wheel open top tramcar number 3. The design of this tram was entirely Claude's, though it was made to look like a typical old style open top tramcar. As it was not modelled on a prototype tram it was give the number 3, being the third tramcar to be built by Claude.

The move to Eastbourne meant a need for two more tramcars and work started on them.

First was number 226, another tram based on the Blackpool Boat, so was given the next number up from 225, but was recorded as number 4.

Number 238 was based on the Blackpool Balloon design and was given one of those numbers (they were numbered 237 to 249) and again recorded as number 5.

Then came the idea to build an extra tramcar for Rhyl. This was another freelance design and was the sixth tramcar, so gained the number 6. In fact it was a quickie, so was actually completed before 226 and 238. When a new design of car was developed for Eastbourne the chassis of number 6 was used. As it was not based on any other tramcar it retained its personal number 6.

The next tramcar used the design of number 6 as a basis and was numbered 7.

The next tramcar to be built was another one based on the Blackpool Boat. By this time number 23 had gone to Scotland and the other three small trams had been withdrawn from service. So Claude gave the new Boat the number 4, rather than a Blackpool number.

Around this period number 226 had been stripped of its Boat body and had become a flat bed works tramcar. This was the first car of the tramway and so was given the number 01.

The next tramcar was the copy of the MET tramcar. This was completed in 1964 and the previous year 3, 225 and 238 had been sold and taken to America. So Claude decided to fill in a gap in the numbering system by using number 2.

When the all-weather single deck tramcar was built Claude had decided that he would reserve the numbers 8-11 inclusive for open top double deck cars of the Eastbourne style. So the single deck car was given the number 12.

Then another tramcar of the open top Eastbourne design was built and became number 8.

The body of MET tramcar 94 was rebuilt into a single deck tram suitable for Seaton and with an acknowledgement to the original number it became 14.

A similar view was taken when the body of Bournemouth 106 was used for a new single deck tram and this became 16.

To allow disabled passengers, particularly those in wheelchairs, to have the opportunity to ride the tramway a new car was built with disabled access. It has a similar design to the open crossbench cars used on the Manx Electric Railway. This was given the next number after 16 and so became 17.

When the body of Exeter 19 was used to make a new single deck tramcar it was natural to allow it to keep its original number and so became 19.

The three new tramcars built in 2002 were updated versions of the old Eastbourne design and so used the reserved numbers 9, 10 and 11.

The final number is one that has been allocated but not yet used. 27 might become a trailer for car 17, in the style of the Manx Electric summer sets following the Manx numbering system.

So the numbering system is:

| 1 | 23 |
|---|---|
| 2(i) | 225 |
| 2(ii) | 2 |
| 3 | 3 |
| 4(i) | 226 |
| 4(ii) | 4 |
| 5 | 238 |
| 6 | 6 |
| 7 | 7 |
| 8 | 8 |
| 9 | 9 |
| 10 | 10 |
| 11 | 11 |
| 12 | 12 |
| 13 | not used |
| 14 | 14 MET 94 |
| 15 | not used |
| 16 | 16 Bournemouth 106 |
| 17 | 17 Disabled car |
| 18 | not used |
| 19 | Exeter 19 |
| 27 | 27 Allocated, not yet used |

In looking in more detail at the individual tramcars, a chronological order has been chosen, using the date when the tram was first in passenger service. In some cases the construction of the tramcar extended over many years. Indeed the construction time for one or two trams was such that other trams were started and completed during that time. Where this has happened it is recorded in the notes for each entry.

# The Passenger Tramcars

## NUMBER 23

**Type:** Bogie, double deck, enclosed streamline design.
**Date built:** 1948/49.
**Date withdrawn:** 1957, sold 1958.
**Built by:** Lancaster Electrical Company works, East Barnet.
**Gauge:** 15 inches.
**Voltage:** 60 volts.
**Controllers:** Sharp.
**Seating capacity:** 23 children.
**Length:** 14 feet
**Width:** 2 feet 8inches
**Motors:** 2 x 1HP.
**Trucks:** Maximum traction.

**Notes:**
This was the first tramcar built by Claude Lane and started with a chalk outline drawn on the workshop door showing how much room was needed in the cab to accommodate Claude. The design and tram number come from the two English Electric built tramcars numbers 23 and 24 made for the Darwen tramway system and later sold to the Llandudno and Colwyn Bay Electric Railway.

Number 23 ran in the yard of the Barnet factory and at fêtes in North London before being taken to St Leonards for the 1951 season. In 1952 it was taken to Voryd park, Rhyl where it ran until the tramway was closed in 1957. It was moved back to the Barnet factory. It was not suitable for re-gauging to 2 feet, so remained in store in the factory.

In 1958 the decision to move completely to Eastbourne had been made and 23 was of no use because it was the wrong gauge. So it was sold to Ian Cormack, then secretary to the Scottish Tramway

**Car 23 at a fete carrying lots of children.** *Seaton Tramway collection.*

**Car 23 in the Liverpool large objects store repainted in a Liverpool style livery.** *Seaton Tramway collection.*

**Car 23 in Cambuslang ready for its journey to Liverpool.** *Photograph Brian Martin.*

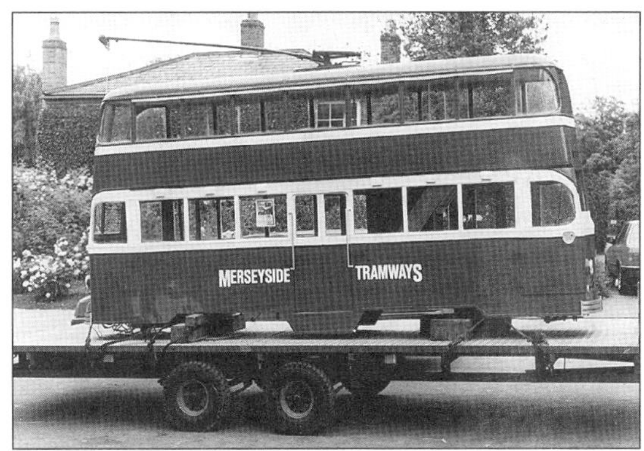


**While in Liverpool car 23 took part in several Lord Mayor parades, on the back of a lorry. Here the Liverpool style livery is very evident.** *Seaton Tramway collection.*

Museum Society (now Scottish Tramway and Transport Society). It left the Barnet factory in June 1958 and was transported to Ian's house in Cambuslang, with the intention of laying track and running it as the only operating tram in Scotland. Although number 23 was joined by the body of Glasgow number 1017, the school training car, the scheme did not go ahead and number 23 spent its time stored in Ian's garage, never having been used. In 1985 Ian moved house and was not able to continue to accommodate the tramcar. It was donated to the Merseyside Tramway Preservation Society and on 16th March 1985 Brian Martin, helped by six members of the STMS, loaded it onto a trailer and he drove it back to Liverpool.

The MTPS also intended to lay track and operate the tramcar. Liverpool was an appropriate location because the later streamline Liverpool tramcars had a broadly similar design to number 23. Initially the tramcar was stored at Speke (now John Lennon) Airport. Later space was found in the Liverpool Council Museum's Large Objects Store Princes Dock. Here it was undergoing restoration along with real Liverpool tramcars. It had been given a repaint with the fleetname "MerseysideTramways". Unfortunately the Council had to close the Large Objects Store and a temporary home was found for all the tramcars in Cammell Laird's Shipyard, Birkenhead. At this time the Birkenhead Council were working with the Merseyside Tramway Preservation Society on the development of the Birkenhead Heritage Tramway. While two new

**Car 23 today in Penketh.** *Photograph authors.*

tramcars were purchased from Hong Kong, it was also the intention to run other tramcars as they were restored by the group. Indeed open top car Birkenhead number 20, enclosed double deck tramcar Liverpool number 762 and balcony top car Wallasey number 78 are now in service. The opportunity to run full size tramcars meant that the idea of building the miniature tramway for number 23 was shelved. Indeed the tramcar now no longer fitted into the development plans. It had no historical connections to the Merseyside area and was surplus to requirements.

Denis Butler, a member of the MPTS, had a great interest in the small tramcar. He first had contact with it when he was a small boy. He would spend his summer holidays with an Aunt who lived in Rhyl. He had come across Voryd Park when it had the miniature steam railway. So he was extremely surprised one year when, as the bus taking him from the station to his Aunt's house drove past Voryd Park, he saw number 23 parked waiting for passengers. From then onward he would badger his Aunt and Uncle to take him to Voryd Park so he could ride the trams. Indeed his Uncle commented that he was funding the Park from the tram fares he paid for the rides Denis had. With such a long association Denis wanted to see 23 continue to have a good home. So he expressed an interest and so ownership was transferred to him in 1994 and he moved 23 to his back garden. A special tram shed was built for the tramcar (getting planning permission for a tram depot confused the local Council); track was laid in the garden; and the tramcar restored back to as close to its original condition as practical. This included repainting the body to the original livery, with transfers made by Stan Letts (maker of all the transfers for Modern Electric Tramway Company trams) and applied on the 4th October 1997. Space in the cabs was extremely cramped, to the extent that the fuller figure of today's tram enthusiast would not fit in. Eric Thornton, a noted tramway modeller, volunteered to make two of his one third scale controllers for the tram. Eric developed these for driving his 1:32 scale tramway and he had special controller tops cast in brass. The new controllers matched the scale of the tramcar and are significantly smaller than the original controllers developed by Claude Lane back in 1948. Denis also removed the handbrake handles. These protruded across the cab doorway making access exceedingly difficult. These two changes even allow a portly author to manage to get into the cab. When the restoration was completed Denis invited Allan Gardner to visit his house and see number 23 again. Allan took up the offer and went to see the tramcar running in the garden. His first reaction was amazement at how small the tramcar was. He could only just get into it to drive it again. He wondered how he managed to hop in and out of it when he was driving it at Rhyl.

On 15th July 1995 number 23 was taken down to Seaton as part of the Silver Jubilee celebrations of the tramway. It was on display at Colyton terminus.

# NUMBER 225

**Type:** Bogie, single deck, open Boat (luxury Toastrack) design.
**Date built:** 1950, rebuilt 1952/53 to a larger size.
**Date withdrawn:** 1957, Sold 1963 to America.
**Built by:** Lancaster Electrical Company works, East Barnet.
**Gauge:** 15 inches, re-gauged in 1954 to 2 feet.
**Voltage:** 60 volts.
**Controllers:** DB1 copy, built at Barnet.
**Seating capacity:** 12.
**Length:** 17 feet 6 inches (after rebuilding).
**Width:** 3 feet 1 inch (after rebuilding).
**Motors:** 2 x 1HP.
**Trucks:** Maximum traction.

**Notes:**
Number 225 was the second tramcar to be built by Claude. Having seen many adults wanting a ride on the miniature tramcar and seeing how difficult it was for them to get into number 23, he chose a design that would be much easier for larger people. His driving experience at Blackpool meant that he was very familiar with the open boat tramcars and knew how popular they were with visitors in the summer season. So he used this as a basis for his new tramcar. This class of tram was numbered 225 to 236 (later 600 to 607). Claude chose the first number, 225, for his tram, probably not realising that this was the first to be built and was slightly different from the others.

Number 225 entered service in May 1950. It appeared to have a much smaller seating capacity than number 23. But the seating for the first tram was based on children and the second on adult passengers. Having no roof meant adults could stand freely in the tramcar. It went to St Leonards with number 23 for the 1951 season and then was taken to Rhyl. The popularity of the miniature trams at Rhyl was such that Claude decided to give a bit more room for passengers and during the winter of 1952/53 the tram body was rebuilt with an extra few inches to its length and width. It

**Car 225 at St Leonards with Geoff Clarke driving.** *Seaton Tramway collection.*

returned to Rhyl for the 1953 season and then in September was moved to Eastbourne. Here it was re-gauged to 2 feet in readiness for the 1954 season. It ran at Eastbourne until 1957 when it was retired as being too small for the demands of the tramway. With numbers 3 and 238 it was sold to Mr Don Sorenson of Wilton, Connecticut in 1963 and shipped to America in the November.

# NUMBER 3

**Type:** Four wheel, open top, double deck.
**Date built:** 1952.
**Date withdrawn:** 1955/6, Sold 1963 to America.
**Built by:** Lancaster Electrical Company works, East Barnet.
**Gauge:** 15 inches, re-gauged in 1954 to 2 feet.
**Voltage:** 60 volts.
**Controllers:** Sharp.
**Seating capacity:** 20.
**Length:** 10 feet
**Width:** 3 feet
**Motors:** 2 x 2.25HP.
**Trucks:** Four wheel.

**Notes:**
Number 3 was built following comments from the public that they would like to see a traditional type of tramcar. So Claude built number 3 using a photograph of a Gosport and Fareham tramcar as inspiration. When it went into service at Rhyl it became the most popular tramcar. It was exactly what the public felt a tram should look like. But there was a major problem – it was too small to meet the demand. When it went to Eastbourne this proved even more of a problem and it was taken out of service at the earliest opportunity. With numbers 225 and 238 it was sold to Mr Don Sorenson of Wilton, Connecticut in 1963 and shipped to America in the November.

**Car 3 at Rhyl.** *Photograph D. Tate.*

# NUMBER 6 (i)

**Type:** Bogie, single deck toastrack design.
**Date built:** 1954.
**Date withdrawn:** 1956 (rebuilt see Number 6 (ii) 1956).
**Built by:** Lancaster Electrical Company works, East Barnet.
**Gauge:** 15 inches.
**Voltage:** 60 volts.
**Controllers:** DB1 K3.
**Seating capacity:** 24.
**Length:** 20 feet.
**Width:** 3 feet.
**Motors:** 2 x 2HP.
**Trucks:** Maximum traction.

**Notes:**
When Claude obtained the concession to operate the tramway at Eastbourne the Twigdens wanted to continue operation of the Rhyl tramway and did so for another three seasons. The agreement was that Modern Electric Tramways supplied the trams and track and maintained the system. But they needed trams to commence running at Eastbourne. So numbers 3 and 225 were taken from Rhyl to Eastbourne. This left only number 23 at Rhyl. Claude was concerned that this would not be sufficient, so the Lancaster Electrical factory built an extra tram as quickly as possible. This was number 6 which was made to a simple open toastrack design, basically a flat floor with seats and a small dash at each end. Construction was undertaken at the same time as 226 and 238, indeed these two trams were started before number 6, but as the latter was so simple it was completed before the other two.

As explained in the text the Twigdens were unimpressed by number 6. Claude had to offer the tram at no extra cost. It actually only operated for one season. It was then taken back to Barnet and it was rebuilt for use at Eastbourne; see number 6(ii) 1956.

**A rare photograph of car 6 as a cross bench tramcar.** *Photograph Brian Martin.*

## NUMBER 226

**Type:** Bogie, single deck, open Boat (luxury Toastrack) design.
**Date built:** 1954.
**Date withdrawn:** 1960 and rebuilt as works car number 01.
**Built by:** Lancaster Electrical Company works, East Barnet.
**Gauge:** 2 feet.
**Voltage:** 60 volts.
**Controllers:** DB1 copy, built at Barnet.
**Seating capacity:** 12.
**Length:** 17 feet 6 inches.
**Width:** 3 feet 3 inches.
**Motors:** 2 x 1HP.
**Trucks:** Maximum traction.

**Notes:**
Number 226 was built using the same basic design as 225 and indeed was given the next number as used in Blackpool. Actually advantage was taken to make it slightly larger than 225 by extending the width by two inches. This follows the general pattern of each new tramcar being larger than the ones before. In 1960 the tram was withdrawn and the chassis and electrical equipment used to make a flat bed works car number 01, that could carry rail and other material around the tramway. This was later rebuilt into the tram shop, then a works car.

**Car 226 at Eastbourne.** *Photograph Ron Howes.*

## NUMBER 238

**Type:** Bogie, double deck style (see below), enclosed streamline “Blackpool Balloon” design.
**Date built:** 1955.
**Date withdrawn:** 1957, Sold 1963 to America.
**Built by:** Lancaster Electrical Company works, East Barnet.
**Gauge:** 2 feet.
**Voltage:** 60 volts.
**Controllers:** DB1 copy, built at Barnet.
**Seating capacity:** 18 adults and 6 children.
**Length:** 21 feet 6 inches.
**Width:** 3 feet 6 inches.
**Motors:** 2 x 2HP.
**Trucks:** Maximum traction.

**Notes:**
In hindsight it was acknowledged that the design of number 238 was a mistake. Claude again took his inspiration from Blackpool. This time he used the streamlined design of the Balloon trams to construct a double deck looking tramcar. Externally it looked like a normal enclosed double deck tramcar, but inside passengers found that there was no upper deck floor. The whole of the inside was open, except for short shelf-like floors above the driving cab. These could be reached by short ladders and were only suitable for children. In use the public were disappointed to find that what they thought was a double deck car was in fact a single deck. It was also a larger car but had quite limited capacity. As soon as the newer cars numbers 6 and 7 were built it was relegated to the back of the depot, only being used in emergencies. With numbers 3 and 225 it was sold to Mr Don Sorenson of Wilton, Connecticut in 1963 and shipped to America in the November.

**Car 238 at Eastbourne terminus.** *Seaton Tramway collection.*

# NUMBER 6 (ii)

**Type:** Bogie, double deck open top, lower deck open cross bench design.
**Date built:** Originally built as number 6 (i) in 1954, see that entry. Chassis used to build a new number 6 in 1956, re-built 1962 with small saloons at each end, rebuilt 1989 to original open cross bench lower deck.
**Date withdrawn:** Still in use.
**Built by:** Lancaster Electrical Company works, East Barnet.
**Gauge:** 2 feet, re-gauged in 1974 to 2 feet 9 inches.
**Voltage:** 60 volts, later 120 volts.
**Controllers:** DB1 K3 B.
**Seating capacity:** 40.
**Length:** 22 feet 6 inches.
**Width:** 4 feet.
**Motors:** 2 x 10HP.
**Trucks:** Maximum traction.

**Notes:**
The popularity of the tramway at Eastbourne meant that there was an urgent need for extra tramcars and ones that were larger than the earlier designs. It was felt that it was the time to design a tramcar specifically to meet the needs of Eastbourne and not to copy an existing tram design. Claude designed a tramcar that had the essential open top, he enclosed the driver's cab with a vestibule (windscreen) and made it easier to get in and out of the lower deck by making it an open cross bench design. So there was immediate access to each seat. The result was a great success. The tram would load and unload quickly, it had a high capacity (40 seats), the only disadvantage being that there was no sheltered accommodation for really wet weather. So in 1962 it was rebuilt with small saloons at each end of the lower deck. When the car went to Seaton and more trams were built, it was decided that the tramcar could be rebuilt to its original form, to encourage passengers to ride on the lower deck. The saloons were removed in 1989.

The controllers came from Southampton tramcar number 81. The top deck seats and scrollwork came from the L&CBER (ex-Bournemouth) tram number 8. The headlights, gongs, bells and circuit breakers came from other L&CBER trams.

**Car 6 with rebuilt ends, giving a small saloon at each end.** *Photograph Dennis Felton.*

**Car 6, built on the chassis of the cross bench car and the first tram designed specifically for Eastbourne.** *Seaton Tramway collection.*

# NUMBER 7

**Type:** Bogie, double deck open top, lower deck open cross bench design.
**Date built:** 1958.
**Date withdrawn:** Still in use.
**Built by:** Lancaster Electrical Company works, East Barnet, completed by Modern Electric Tramways, Eastbourne.
**Gauge:** 2 feet, re-gauged in 1976 to 2 feet 9 inches.
**Voltage:** 60 volts, later 120 volts.
**Controllers:** DB1 K3 B.
**Seating capacity:** 37.
**Length:** 22 feet 6 inches.
**Width:** 4 feet 2 inches.
**Motors:** 2 x 10HP.
**Trucks:** Maximum traction.

**Notes:**
Following the success of the design of number 6, the next tramcar to be built was made to the same design, except it had small saloons at each end of the lower deck and was made 2 inches wider, to give a little more room for passengers.

Like number 6 the top deck seats, headlights, gongs, bells and circuit breakers all came from the L&CBER. The controllers came from L&CBER (ex-Accrington) tram number 3 and the seats in the small saloons came from Leeds.

**Car 7 at Eastbourne.** *Photograph Geoff Tribe.*

# NUMBER 4

**Type:** Bogie, single deck, open Boat (luxury Toastrack) design.
**Date built:** 1961.
**Date withdrawn:** Still in service.
**Built by:** Modern Electric Tramways, Eastbourne.
**Gauge:** 2 feet, re-gauged in 1976 to 2 feet 9 inches.
**Voltage:** 120 volts.
**Controllers:** DB1 K33E.
**Seating capacity:** 20.
**Length:** 28 feet 6 inches.
**Width:** 4 feet 6 inches.
**Motors:** 2 x 10HP.
**Trucks:** Maximum traction.

**Notes:**
This is the third open Boat that has been built by the company. Once again it was larger than the other two and is still in service. Built for Eastbourne it had a specific role. It was built to be able to take standing passengers. So when it reached the Crumbles terminus, if the seats were full and no one wanted to alight, it was still able to pick up waiting passengers. It has also developed a role as the tramcar that can be fitted with lights for celebrations. Strings of bulbs are fitted from the trolley tower to poles fitted at the ends of the tram.

The motorman's air brake valves, air whistles, controllers and circuit breakers came from the Darwen trams that went to the L&CBER. It has seats and air compressors from Glasgow trams. The trolley equipment comes from Sheffield.

For a short while in 1974 it was fitted with an experimental Brecknell Willis single arm pantograph. The pantograph design was subsequently used on main line electric locomotives.

**The third 'Boat' design car 4 at Eastbourne.** *Photograph Gordon Gangloff.*

# NUMBER 2

**Type:** Bogie, open top, uncanopied, double deck.
**Date built:** 1964.
**Date withdrawn:** Still in service.
**Built by:** Modern Electric Tramways, Eastbourne.
**Gauge:** 2 feet, re-gauged in 1970 to 2 feet 9 inches.
**Voltage:** 60 volts, then in 1960 120 volts.
**Controllers:** DE1 Form B.
**Seating capacity:** 35.
**Length:** 25 feet 6 inches.
**Width:** 4 feet 6 inches.
**Motors:** 2 x 10HP.
**Trucks:** Maximum traction.

**Notes:**
Number 2 was designed using features found on the Metropolitan Electric Tramways Company and the London United Tramways Company. Those used on number 2 were the "Robinson" type stairs, with two short straight stairs and a half landing. It also had elaborate scrollwork railings around the upper deck. While all the previous Modern Electric Tramways cars were finished in green and cream liveries, number two was given the Metropolitan red and white livery. Like many of the other trams built by Modern Electric Tramways it incorporates many parts from actual tramcars that once ran in Britain.

The upper deck seats were once used by the Grimsby and Immingham trams, the tram gongs were from London Transport E/3 number 179, some of the panels came from trams from Glasgow and the L&CBER. The circuit breakers and brake handles also came from Glasgow, while the controllers once drove Wallasey trams.

**Car 2 at Seaton.** *Photograph authors.*

# NUMBER 12

**Type:** Bogie, single deck, fully enclosed; later double deck, open top.
**Date built:** 1966, rebuilt 1980 and 1999.
**Date withdrawn:** Still in use.
**Built by:** Modern Electric Tramways, Eastbourne.
**Gauge:** 2 feet, re-gauged in 1971 to 2 feet 9 inches.
**Voltage:** 120 volts.
**Controllers:** DB1 K33E.
**Seating capacity:** 20, after 1980 rebuild 50.
**Length:** 1966 – 31 feet 6 inches. 1999 – 33 feet.
**Width:** 4 feet 10 inches.
**Motors:** 2 x 10HP.
**Trucks:** Equal Wheel.

**Notes:**
Number 12 is the most rebuilt tramcar in the fleet. Built originally for Eastbourne it was made as a totally enclosed single deck car with equal wheel bogies. It was equipped with heating for use on cold wet days or the colder evenings. The tramcar was designed with doors on both sides at both ends, to allow for one man operation during quieter periods.The controllers of the tramcar came from one of the ex-Darwen tramcars at the Llandudno & Colwyn Bay Electric Railway, seats are from the Leeds tramway, some windows from Glasgow and the trolley is ex-Sheffield. In June 1974 the tram was commissioned by Brecknell-Willis to test their new single arm pantograph. In 1978 it was decided to rebuild the tramcar by putting an open top on to it and opening the lower saloon in the "Eastbourne" style. This more than doubled the seating capacity. Then in 1999 it was decided to restyle the tramcar by fitting "Feltham" style driver cabs. The tramcar was repainted in a London Transport style livery. While no open top "Feltham" tramcars were ever built, if they had this is what they would have looked like! The styling is so good that many visitors who can remember the London trams actually think it is a real London tram.

**The first design of car 12, here at Eastbourne.** *Photograph D N Warren.*

**Car 12 at Seaton during the experimental pantograph period.** *Seaton Tramway collection.*

**Car 12 during reconstruction into an open top double deck tram, on Riverside curve.** *Seaton Tramway collection.*

**The final version of car 12 with the Feltham style cabs and sporting a London style livery.** *Photograph authors.*

# NUMBER 8

**Type:** Bogie, double deck open top, lower deck open cross bench design with small saloons.
**Date built:** 1968, rebuilt 1992 removing the saloons and replacing with open cross bench seating.
**Date withdrawn:** Still in use.
**Built by:** Modern Electric Tramways, Eastbourne.
Gauge: 2 feet, re-gauged in 1970 to 2 feet 9 inches.
**Voltage:** 120 volts.
**Controllers:** DB1 K3.
**Seating capacity:** 41.
**Length:** 25 feet 6 inches.
**Width:** 4 feet 6 inches.
**Motors:** 2 x 10HP.
**Trucks:** Maximum traction.

**Notes:**
Number 8 was built after the decision had been made to move to Seaton. So while it was built to the principles of the "Eastbourne" design, it is three feet longer and 4-6 inches wider than numbers 6 and 7 to meet the wider gauge. It had the honour of being the first paying passenger carrying tramcar at Seaton when it ran using a battery trailer to power it.

**Car 8 at Colyford, before the tramway crossed the road.** *Photograph Geoff Tribe.*

**Car 8 with the end saloons removed and the lower deck all cross bench.** *Photograph John H Meredith.*

# NUMBER 14

**Type:** Bogie, single deck, fully enclosed.
**Date built:** 1984.
**Date withdrawn:** Still in use.
**Built by:** Modern Electric Tramways, Eastbourne and Seaton.
**Gauge:** 2 feet 9 inches.
**Voltage:** 120 volts.
**Controllers:** GEC K10.
**Seating capacity:** 26.
**Length:** 30 feet 6 inches.
**Width:** 5 feet 4 inches.
**Motors:** 2 x 10HP.
**Trucks:** Maximum Traction.

**Ex MET car 94 prior to restoration and rebuilding as car 14. This clearly shows the condition of the saloon and the amount of work necessary.** *Photograph John Wills.*

**Notes:**
The body of London Transport 2455 (MET 94) was found by a group of enthusiasts in 1960 at Waltham Cross. The tramcar had been built in 1904 as an open top bogie car. It ran on the Metropolitan Electric Tramway system and then for London Transport, being withdrawn in 1935. When the enthusiasts acquired the car they moved it to the Eastbourne tramway in 1961 with the intention of rebuilding it to its 1904 condition. Progress was slow and in 1968 ownership of the tram passed to Modern Electric Tramways. It was decided that the body should be used to build a tramcar for the narrow gauge tramway. So the lower saloon was narrowed by cutting down the middle, removing a section and joining the sides back together. The tramcar was painted in the red and white livery of the Metropolitan Electric Tramways Limited. The rebuilding of the original standard gauge body took a long time due to the move to Seaton. The seating is a combination of single garden seats on one side and longitudinal seating on the other side. It entered service on 2 June 1984. As its old MET number was 94 it was decided to number the car 14. It is very large when seen next to the standard tramcars.

**Car 14 under construction at Seaton the body shows the use of the original Metropolitan Electric Tramways body.** *Seaton Tramway collection.*

**The finished car 14 at Seaton terminus.** *Seaton Tramway collection.*

# NUMBER 17

**Type:** Bogie, single deck, open cross bench.
**Date built:** 1988.
**Date withdrawn:** Still in use.
**Built by:** Modern Electric Tramways, Seaton.
**Gauge:** 2 feet 9 inches.
**Voltage:** 120 volts.
**Controllers:** DB1 Form B.
**Seating capacity:** 48.
**Length:** 30 feet 6 inches.
**Width:** 5 feet 6 inches.
**Motors:** 2 x 10HP.
**Trucks:** Maximum Traction.

**Notes:**
From the start of operation at Seaton the number of passengers carried on the tramway increased each year. During the 1980s it became apparent that many of the visitors were people in wheelchairs. The tramway did its best to accommodate these passengers, but some of the more frail were unable to be helped into the lower decks of the existing tramcars. So it was decided to build a tramcar that could be converted to carry wheelchairs. The result was number 17. It was styled on the crossbench tramcars running on the Manx Electric Railway on the Isle of Man. It was fitted with crossbench seats that can be removed. By using a dedicated ramp wheelchairs can be rolled up onto the tram and they fit in the space left after removal of the seats. Up to 12 passengers in wheelchairs with 10 helpers can be carried.

**The disabled access car 17 at the new Seaton terminus.** *Photograph John H Meredith.*

# NUMBER 16

**Type:** Bogie, single deck, fully enclosed.
**Date built:** 1992.
**Date withdrawn:** Still in use.
**Built by:** Modern Electric Tramways, Seaton.
**Gauge:** 2 feet 9 inches.
**Voltage:** 120 volts.
**Controllers:** DB1 K4B.
**Seating capacity:** 26.
**Length:** 32 feet 6 inches.
**Width:** 5 feet 8 inches.
**Motors:** 2 x 10HP.
**Trucks:** Maximum Traction.

**Notes:**
Bournemouth Transport Preservation Group found the body of Bournemouth tramcar number 106 in 1974. The Group presented it to Seaton Tramway. It was decided to use the lower saloon to build a new tram for Seaton. A similar conversion to number 14 was carried out. The tramcar was painted in the old Bournemouth maroon and cream livery.

**Car 16 under construction with the original Bournemouth body.** *Seaton Tramway collection.*

**At Colyton car 16 gets ready for another trip.** *Photograph authors.*

## NUMBER 19

**Type:** Bogie, single deck, totally enclosed.
**Date built:** 1998.
**Date withdrawn:** Still in use.
**Built by:** Modern Electric Tramways, Seaton.
**Gauge:** 2 feet 9 inches.
**Voltage:** 120 volts.
**Controllers:** DB1 K4.
**Seating capacity:** 20.
**Length:** 26 feet.
**Width:** 5 feet 10 inches.
**Motors:** 2 x 10HP.
**Trucks:** Maximum Traction.

**Notes:**
Another actual tram body that was used by Modern Electric Tramways was Exeter Corporation Tramways number 19 (later renumbered 21). In 1984 the body found in Rewe and was donated to the Mid Devon Tramway Preservation Society. However, they were unable to take on the project of restoring the car. It was subsequently rescued by Colin Shears of the West of England Transport Collection and it was donated to Seaton in 1994. A similar conversion to numbers 14 and 16 was carried out. As the original tram carried the number 19 and it fitted in well with the sequence it retained its number. It was painted in the green and white livery carried by the tram in its Exeter days.

**The body of Exeter car 19 was used to make car 19.** *Photograph authors.*

## NUMBER 9

**Type:** Bogie, double deck open top, drop centre lower deck.
**Date built:** 2002.
**Date withdrawn:** Still in use.
**Built by:** Bolton Trams, Wigan.
**Gauge:** 2 feet 9 inches.
**Voltage:** 120 volts.
**Controllers:** DB1 K3.
**Seating capacity:** 56.
**Length:** 33 feet.
**Width:** 5 feet.
**Motors:** 4 x 6HP.
**Trucks:** Maximum traction.

**Notes:**
This is the first tramcar not to be built by either Claude Lane or Modern Electric Tramways and is one of a batch of three trams ordered in 2001. The body was built by Bolton Trams in their Wigan workshop and has a hexagonal type of dash panel. The tramcar was fitted out in the Seaton workshops, with seats from the Grimsby and Immingham Tramway; controllers from Lisbon and trucks made by Modern Electric Tramways. Number 9 is painted in a two tone blue livery. It was publicised as representing the Birmingham livery, but it is not meant to be an accurate representation.

**Car 9 in the paint shop receiving its blue livery.** *Photograph authors.*

## NUMBER 10

**Type:** Bogie, double deck open top, drop centre lower deck.
**Date built:** 2002.
**Date withdrawn:** Still in use.
**Built by:** Bolton Trams, Wigan.
**Gauge:** 2 feet 9 inches.
**Voltage:** 120 volts.
**Controllers:** DB1 K3.
**Seating capacity:** 56.
**Length:** 33 feet.
**Width:** 5 feet.
**Motors:** 4 x HP.
**Trucks:** Maximum traction.

**Notes:**
The second of three trams ordered from Bolton Trams. Like number 9 it was fitted out in the Seaton workshops, with seats from the Grimsby and Immingham Tramway; controllers from Lisbon and trucks made by Modern Electric Tramways. Number 10 is painted in a green, cream and orange livery. It was publicised as representing the Glasgow livery, but it is not meant to be an accurate representation.

**In the paint shop car 10 gets its lining and lettering.** *Photograph authors.*

## NUMBER 11

**Type:** Bogie, double deck open top, drop centre lower deck.
**Date built:** 2002.
**Date withdrawn:** Still in use.
**Built by:** Bolton Trams, Wigan.
**Gauge:** 2 feet 9 inches.
**Voltage:** 120 volts.
**Controllers:** DB1 K3.
**Seating capacity:** 56.
**Length:** 33 feet.
**Width:** 5 feet.
**Motors:** 4 x HP.
**Trucks:** Maximum traction.

**Notes:**
The last of the three trams ordered from Bolton Trams. Like number 9 it was fitted out in the Seaton workshops, with seats from the Grimsby and Immingham Tramway, controllers from Lisbon and trucks made by Modern Electric Tramways. Number 11 is painted in a two tone cream livery. It was publicised as representing the Liverpool First Class Car livery, but it is not meant to be an accurate representation.

**Car 11 in its bare metal state waits for its turn in the paint shop.** *Photographs authors.*

# NUMBER 27

**Type:** Bogie, single deck, cross bench seating.
**Date built:** Under construction.
**Date withdrawn:** N/a.
**Built by:** Modern Electric Tramways, Seaton.
**Gauge:** 2 feet 9 inches.
**Voltage:** N/a.
**Controllers:** N/a.
**Seating capacity:** Not known.
**Length:** 30 feet 6 inches.
**Width:** 5 feet 6 inches.
**Motors:** N/a.
**Trucks:** Not known.

**Notes:**
Number 27 was planned to be a trailer car for number 17, in the style of the Manx Electric Railway. A frame was started some years ago as a welding exercise. It has been parked on the siding at Colyford for some years with no further work carried out on it. Hopefully at some time it will be taken on again and a matching trailer for number 17 will be made.

**The framework to be seen at Colyford. This was due to become a trailer 27 to car 17. Now the tramway has other plans.** *Photograph authors.*

# THE TRAM THAT ONLY CAME FOR A VISIT

In addition to the fleet detailed above the tramway has had a visit from one other tramcar. However, though it was on site for over a year, the tram never turned a wheel on the rails. Indeed for much of its stay the truck was separated from the body of the car. The tram was Lisbon number 730. Purchased privately from the Lisbon tramway there were plans for the tram to be regauged from its 900mm gauge to the Seaton 2ft 9in. However these did not materialise and the tram spent its stay on the tramway parked on the other side of the wall at Colyton. Eventually the tram was taken away and any thoughts of it running at Seaton were put away.

**Lisbon 730 at Colyton during its visit to the tramway.**

# The Works Tramcars

## TRAM 02

**Type:** Four wheel totally enclosed car, then bogie totally enclosed with overhead platform.
**Date built:** 1952, rebuilt 1968, rebuilt 1992.
**Date withdrawn:** Still in use.
**Built by:** Lancaster Electrical Company works, East Barnet, rebuilt Modern Electric Tramways, Eastbourne, second rebuild Modern Electric Tramways, Seaton.
**Gauge:** 2 feet, re-gauged 1973 to 2 feet 9 inches.
**Voltage:** 120 volts, later unpowered trailer.
**Controllers:** BTH 510 ex Lisbon.
**Length:** 18 feet 6 inches.
**Width:** 4 feet.
**Motors:** 2 x 10HP.
**Trucks:** Four wheel, then Maximum Traction.

**Notes:**
This tram was commissioned in 1952 by the Air Ministry as a battery operated 2ft gauge single deck four wheel tramcar. The completion was delayed by changing specifications from the Air Ministry. The tram was moved to Eastbourne in 1958 and work continued on the almost completed tram. Then the Air Ministry cancelled the order. At Eastbourne the tram was used for works duties helping with the relaying of track. It was then put in store at Eastbourne. In 1968 the tram was taken out of store and the body lengthened by one bay. It was fitted with an overhead gantry and mounted on standard bogies. It was used to erect the overhead on the Seaton tramway. In the winter of 1981 it was blown over in a gale and the body badly damaged. The body was rebuilt with larger platforms and hexagonal dashes and lightweight trailer bogies fitted. So the car was now a trailer. However, it was realised that an overhead car was required because demands for maintenance on both the track and overhead grew. The car was given new motor bogies in 1992. The tram has ex Grimsby & Immingham controllers.

**Works car 02, as built for the Air Ministry and used as a works car when the contract was cancelled.** *Photograph John H Meredith.*

**02 extended and placed on bogies.** *Photograph D.N. Warren.*

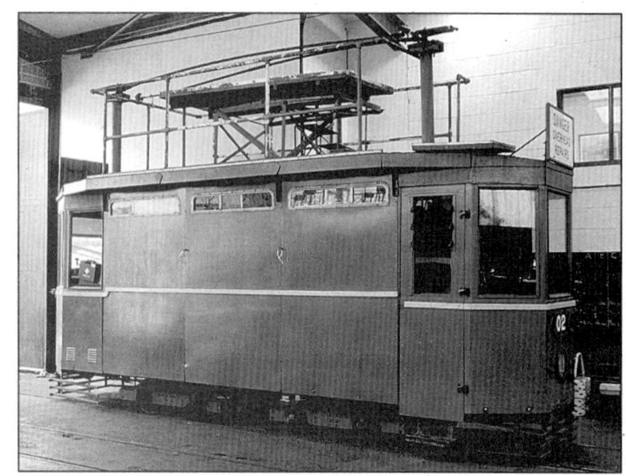
**Waiting in readiness for a call, 02 is in the depot.**

# TRAM 01

**Type:** Flat bed works car, then the tram shop, then ganger's trailer.
**Date built:** 1960, rebuilt 1965, rebuilt 1995.
**Date withdrawn:** Still in use.
**Built by:** Lancaster Electrical Company works, East Barnet, rebuilt Modern Electric Tramways, Eastbourne, second rebuild Modern Electric Tramways, Seaton.
**Gauge:** 2 feet, re-gauged 1973 to 2 feet 9 inches.
**Voltage:** 120 volts, later unpowered trailer.
**Controllers:** DB1 K3.
**Length:** 18 feet 6 inches.
**Width:** 4 feet.
**Motors:** 2 x 10HP.
**Trucks:** Maximum Traction.

**Notes:**
The first works car number 01 was a conversion of open Boat tramcar 226. In 1960 the body was removed and the tramcar fitted with two small dashes and a trolley standard. It became a flat bed car, the most minimal of all tramcars. In this form it was able to carry rails and all kinds of other material around the Eastbourne tramway. Following the spate of break-ins at the sales kiosk, Claude decided to build a shop that could be taken back to the depot at nights. Number 01 was ideal for conversion because it was basically just a chassis. So a single deck enclosed car was built, the saloon being fitted out as a shop, service being provided through a sliding window. The Tram Shop was ready for the start of the 1965 season. It would be driven out at the beginning of the operating day to sell tickets and show that the tramway was running. In addition to tickets it sold souvenirs, postcards, tramway books and models. It fulfilled a similar role at Seaton, particularly when the tramway was extended to the car park. However, the motors and trolley pole were removed and it became a trailer. It was hauled out by the first tram of the day. Electricity was supplied by a lead plugged into a socket on the nearest traction pole. When the new terminus was opened in 1995 a purpose built shop was part of the complex and so the tram shop became redundant. The internal fittings were removed and the tram was converted into a ganger's car, right down to a sink fitted into one of the dashes.

**Car 01 today, as the Staff Wagon trailer.** *Photograph authors.*

**Boat 226 was stripped to its chassis and used as a flat bed works car 01.** *Seaton Tramway collection.*

**The reconstruction of car 01 into the Tram Shop. Claude Lane stands in the doorway.** *Seaton Tramway collection.*

**Car 01 was then rebuilt as the Tram Shop. First motorised and later as a trailer, as in this photograph.** *Photograph authors.*

# TRAM 03

**Type:** Bogie Welding Trailer.
**Date built:** 1986.
**Date withdrawn:** Still in use.
**Built by:** Modern Electric Tramways, Seaton.
**Gauge:** 2 feet 9 inches.
**Voltage:** Unpowered trailer.
**Controllers:** None.
**Length:** 16 feet.
**Width:** 4 feet.
**Motors:** None.
**Trucks:** Lightweight trailing bogies.

**Notes:**
Another work-horse of the maintenance gang. The unit provides a self-contained unit for welding anywhere on the tramway. This is essential for the track and overhead equipment.

**Welding trailer 03.** *Photograph authors.*

# TRAM 04

**Type:** Bogie Hydraulic Hoist trailer.
**Date built:** 1988.
**Date withdrawn:** Still in use.
**Built by:** Modern Electric Tramways, Seaton.
**Gauge:** 2 feet 9 inches.
**Voltage:** Unpowered trailer.
**Controllers:** None.
**Length:** 16 feet.
**Width:** 4 feet.
**Motors:** None.
**Trucks:** Lightweight trailing bogies.

**Notes:**
This fearsome machine has proved invaluable for painting and maintaining the overhead traction poles. It has gained the nickname "the bucket" from the platform at the end of the hoist, which looks very large compared to the rest of the vehicle. This has inevitably led to another nickname of "Hyacinth" from the equally fearsome character in the television show "Keeping Up Appearances".

It can also be fitted with a tank and spraying equipment to become the weed-killer wagon. In this form it provides an effective means of keeping the weeds under control.

**Hydraulic hoist trailer 04 known as the 'Bucket' or by "Keeping Up Appearances" fans as Hyacinth.** *Photograph authors.*

# TRAM 05

**Type:** Four wheel drop-side wagon.
**Date built:** 1988.
**Date withdrawn:** Still in use.
**Built by:** Modern Electric Tramways, Seaton.
**Gauge:** 2 feet 9 inches.
**Voltage:** Unpowered trailer.
**Controllers:** None.
**Length:** 6 feet.
**Width:** 4 feet.
**Motors:** None.
**Trucks:** Four wheel truck.

**Notes:**
General purpose wagon, used to carry all kinds of material for the maintenance of the tramway.

**Drop side wagon 05.** *Photograph authors.*

# WORKS 06

**Type:** Kubota tractor.
**Date built:** 2002.
**Date withdrawn:** Still in use.
**Built by:** Kubota.
**Gauge:** 2 feet 9 inches, using flanged guide wheels.
**Voltage:** Not Applicable.
**Controllers:** None.
**Motors:** Diesel.
**Trucks:** Not Applicable.

**Notes:**
Used for trackwork and hedge cutting duties. Flanged metal wheels have been fitted to the arms carrying the front "bucket". By lowering the "bucket" the front steering wheels are raised. An attachment at the rear allows a further pair of flanged wheels to contact the rails, while the rear rubber wheels are still in contact with the tops of the rails and drive the tractor. By good fortune the rubber wheels match the 2ft 9in. gauge track.

**Kubota tractor is officially numbered 06, but does not carry a number.** *Photograph authors.*

# Other Vehicles

## RUSTON & HORNSBY DIESEL NUMBER 435398

When the extension from the depot to the car park was to be built it was evident that there was much earth moving to do. A ramp had to be constructed to lift the line from the ground level by the field to the railway embankment. This became a 1 in 40 slope using a thousand tons of brick rubble. To help with all this work in 1973 a second-hand 3 feet gauge 0-4-0 diesel was purchased from the North Devon Clay Company, Torrington. It had to have several tons of ballast weights removed and then was regauged to 2 feet 9 inches in the depot workshop. After many years of useful service the locomotive was out of use, parked at Colyton, for many years. It has recently been sold.

**The Ruston and Hornsby diesel. It was recently sold to a railway preservation society.**

## TIP WAGONS

With the purchase of the diesel some tip wagons were bought from a china clay line near Corfe Castle. These were used in the construction of the tramway. It has been very difficult finding photos of these wagons. The only one found is very much in the background. None of the wagons exist complete, though parts are around the depot.

**Photographs of the tipper wagons are exceptionally rare. This is the only view of a tipper wagon, and then it is very much in the background.** *Seaton Tramway collection.*

# 1880 MIDLAND RAILWAY CARRIAGE AND WAGON COMPANY WOODEN OPEN WAGON

This came with the diesel and has since been passed on to railway preservationists.

# FLAT BED WAGONS

The origin of the flat bed wagons is not known. They were around during the construction of the tramway at Seaton. Photographs show them being used to transport rails and sleepers, then in use as the battery trailers. They have continued to be used throughout the whole of the existence of the Seaton and District Tramway.

**The pair of flat trucks used to convey heavy loads like rails and sleepers.** *Photograph authors.*

# DOUBLE DECK OPEN TOP BUS

In 1957 Claude Lane made a scaled down replica of a L.G.O.C. B-type omnibus. It was mounted on a 9HP Swift car chassis, originally built in 1929. The replica carried the fleet number "B339" and was registered as a road vehicle with a licence number LA 9927. The bus was used to promote the Eastbourne Tramway. It was moved to Seaton with all the other Tramway material and in latter years it was stored covered in tarpaulins behind the depot. Recently it has been removed for restoration.

**The scaled down replica L.G.O.C. B-type omnibus, with Claude Lane driving.** *Photograph John Wills.*

# APPENDIX 3

| No. | Body | Gauge | Built | Withdrawn | Length | Width |
|---|---|---|---|---|---|---|
| **PASSENGER CARS** | | | | | | |
| 2 | Open top uncanopied | 2ft then in 1970 2ft 9in | 1964 | | 25ft 6in | 4ft 6in |
| 3 | Open top | 15in then in 1954 2ft | 1952 | 1963 | 10ft 0in | 3ft 0in |
| 4 | Open boat | 2ft then in 1976 2ft 9in | 1961 | | 28ft 6in | 4ft 6in |
| 6 (i) | Toast-rack | 15in | 1954 | 1954 | 20ft approx | 3ft approx |
| 6(ii) | Open top, vestibuled | 2ft then in 1976 2ft 9in | 1956 | | 22ft 6in | 4ft 0in |
| 7 | Open top, vestibuled | 2ft then in 1976 2ft 9in | 1958 | | 22ft 6n | 4ft 2in |
| 8 | Open top, vestibuled | 2ft then in 1970 2ft 9in | 1968 | | 25ft 6in | 4ft 6in |
| 9 | Open top | 2ft 9in | 2003 | | 33ft 0in | 5ft 0in |
| 10 | Open top | 2ft 9in | 2003 | | 33ft 0in | 5ft 0in |
| 11 | Open top | 2ft 9in | 2003 | | 33ft 0in | 5ft 0in |
| 12 | Single deck, enclosed | 2ft then in 1971 2ft 9in | 1966 | 1979 | 31ft 6in | 4ft 10in |
| 12(i) | Open top, vestibuled | 2ft 9in | 1980 | 1999 | 31ft 6in | 4ft 10in |
| 12 (ii) | Double deck vestibuled, 'Feltham' style ends | 2ft 9in | 1999 | | 33ft 0in | 4ft 10in |
| 14 | Single deck, enclosed | 2ft 9in | 1984 | | 30ft 6in | 5ft 4in |
| 16 | Single deck, enclosed | 2ft 9in | 1992 | | 32ft 6in | 5ft 8in |
| 17 | Single deck, crossbench | 2ft 9in | 1988 | | 30ft 6in | 5ft 6in |
| 19 | Single deck, enclosed | 2ft 9in | 1998 | | 26ft | 5ft 10in |
| 23 | Streamlined double deck, totally enclosed | 15in | 1949 | 1957 | 14ft | 2ft 8in |
| 225 | Open boat | 15in then in 1954 2ft | 1950 | 1963 | 17ft 6in | 3ft 1in |
| 226 | Open boat | 2ft | 1954 | 1960 | 17ft 6in | 3ft 3in |
| 238 | Streamline double deck, totally enclosed | 2ft | 1955 | 1963 | 21ft 6in | 3ft 6in |
| **WORKS CARS** | | | | | | |
| 01 (i) | Flat bed works car | 2ft | 1960 | 1964 | 18ft 6in | 3ft 6in |
| 01 (ii) | Shop tramcar | 2ft | 1965 | 1969 | 18ft 6in | 3ft 6in |
| 01 (iii) | Shop trailer | 2ft 9in | 1971 | 1995 | 18ft 6in | 3ft 6in |
| 01 (iv) | Gangers' trailer | 2ft 9in | 2000 | | 18ft 6in | 3ft 6in |
| 02 (i) | O/H works car | 2ft | 1952 | | 20ft | 4ft |
| 02 (ii) | O/H works trailer | 2ft 9in | 1968 | 1981 | 20ft | 4ft |
| 02 (iii) | O/H works car | 2ft 9in | 1982 | | 20ft | 4ft |
| 03 | Welding trailer | 2ft 9in | 1986 | | 16ft | 4ft |
| 04 | Hydraulic hoist trailer | 2ft 9in | 1988 | | 16ft | 4ft |
| 05 | 4-wheel drop-side trailer | 2ft 9in | 1988 | | 6ft | 4ft |
| 06 | Kubota tractor | N/A | 2002 | | | |
| 435398 | Ruston & Hornsby diesel 0-4-0, class 48DL | 2ft 9in re-gauged from 3ft | 1962 | | | |
| | Wooden open wagon | 3ft | 1880 | | | |
| | Tipper wagons | 2ft 9in | 1962 | | | |
| | 2 flat bed wagons | 2ft 9in | circa1962 | | | |

# Modern Electric Tramways Ltd

| Seats | Controllers | Motors | Notes |
|---|---|---|---|
| 35 | DE1 Form B | 2 x 3.75HP | |
| 20 | Sharp | 2 x 2.25HP | Sold to USA in 1963 to Mr Don Sorenson, Wilton, Connecticut. |
| 20 | DB1 K33E | 2 x 3.75HP | |
| 24 | DB1 K3 | 2 x 3.75HP | |
| 39 | DB1 K3B | 2 x 3.75HP | |
| 37 | DB1 K3E | 2 x 3.75HP | |
| 43 | DB1 K4 | 2 x 3.75HP | |
| 56 | DB1 K33 | 4 x 6HP | Body by Bolton trams |
| 56 | DB1 K33 | 4 x 6HP | Body by Bolton trams |
| 56 | DB1 K33 | 4 x 6HP | Body by Bolton trams |
| 20 | DB1 K33E | 2 x 3.75HP | |
| 50 | DB1 K33E | 2 x 3.75HP | |
| 48 | DB1 K33E | 2 x 3.75HP | |
| 27 | GEC K10 | 2 x 8HP | Ex MET 94, built 1904 withdrawn 1935 |
| 27 | DB1 K4B | 2 x 8HP | Ex Bournemouth 106, built 1921 withdrawn 1935 |
| 48 | DE1 Form B | 2 x 8HP | For disabled passengers |
| 20 | DB1 K4 | 2 x 6HP | Ex Exeter 19, built 1906 withdrawn 1931 |
| 23 children | Sharp | | Sold to STMS, then MTPS, now in private ownership |
| 12 | DB1 copy | 2 x 2.25HP | Rebuilt 1952/3. Sold to USA in 1963 to Mr Don Sorenson, Wilton, Connecticut. |
| 12 | DB1 copy | 2 x 2.25HP | Rebuilt as 01 mobile shop and later gangers' trailer (see below). |
| 18 adults & 6 children | DB1 copy | 2 x 2.25HP | Sold to USA in 1963 to Mr Don Sorenson, Wilton, Connecticut. |
| | | | |
| | DB1 copy | | |
| | DB1 copy | | |
| | None | None | |
| | | | |
| | DB1 K3 | | |
| | | | |
| | DB1 K3, replaced with BTH B510 form N controllers in 1998 | 2 x 3.75HP | A trailer until 1992, when the car was repowered using trucks previously under car 16 |
| | | | Rebuilt in 1994 with cover |
| | | | |
| | | | |
| | | | This vehicle has road/rail capability and is fitted with front loader, and rear backhoe and flail mower attachments. |
| | | | Purchased c. 1971 from North Devon Clay Company. Sold to Devon Railway Centre at Bickleigh for restoration in 2002. |
| | | | Purchased with Ruston and Hornsby locomotive and immediately passed on to railway preservationists. |
| | | | Purchased for track building, two have survived, but are in dismantled condition. |
| | | | Believed built by Seaton Tramway, still in use. |

# BIBLIOGRAPHY

Please note that by far the most material was given during interviews with Allan Gardner, Sue Gardner and Mark Horner.


Boylett, L.J.: Eastbourne Tramways, London, Ian Allan, undated, but c.1964

Croft, D.J.: A Survey of Seaside Miniature Railways, Oxford, The Oakwood Press, 1992, ISBN 0853614180

Eastbourne Borough Council Minutes of the Entertainments and Pleasure Grounds Committee, 1953-1968

Harley, R.J.: Seaton and Eastbourne Tramways, Midhurst, Middleton Press, 1996, ISBN 18737993766

Hills, S.M.: Battery Electric Vehicles, London, George Newnes Ltd., 1943

Maggs C.G.: The Seaton Branch and Seaton Tramway, Oxford, The Oakwood Press, 1992, ISBN 0853614253

Modern Electric Tramcars at Eastbourne, souvenir brochure, undated, but c.1954

Old Glory, Number 12 January/February 1991, article "Trams for the Axe" by John Hobbs

Price, J.H.: The Seaton Tramway, London, Light Railway Transport League, undated, but c.1974

Ross Silcock: Seaton Tramway Extension, Feasibility Study, July 2001

Seaton Tramway, souvenir brochure published by The Seaton Tramway, undated, but c.1977

Seaton Tramway, souvenir brochure published by The Seaton Tramway, undated, but c.1980

Seaton Tramway, souvenir brochure published by The Seaton Tramway, 1986

Seaton Tramway, souvenir brochure published by The Seaton Tramway, 1995

The Narrow Gauge, magazine of the Narrow Gauge Railway Society, issue 123, Summer 1989, article "The 15 inch Gauge Rhyl Electric Tramway", by David Holroyde

The Tramway Tribune, the official newspaper of Seaton and District Electric Tramway

Tramfare, magazine of the Tramway and Light Railway Society, various issues

Tramway Review, historical magazine of the Light Rail Transit Association, various issues

Tramways and Urban Transit, magazine of the Light Rail Transit Association, (previously titled Modern Tramway; and Light Rail and Modern Tramway), various issues

# More Transport Titles in the Adam Gordon Collection

## The Definitive Guide to Trams (including funiculars) in The British Isles

**David Voice. Softback, A5, 184pp, covers coloured on both sides, £15.**

"An excellent work of reference, ideal for all tram fans, very well researched and produced and mirrors the growing stature of Adam Gordon's publishing." [Tramfare].

"The author is to be congratulated for amassing such a wealth of information ... highly recommended for all who wish to keep abreast of what is now the fast-changing tramway and light rail scene in Britain and Ireland..." [Tramways & Urban Transit].

"A very handy volume indeed, worth every penny." [TMS]

## Double Deck Trams of the World, Beyond the British Isles

**Brian Patton, A4 softback, 180pp, covers coloured both sides, £18.**

"Patton has searched far and wide for his material, down to the photographic record of the only double-decker ever to run in Zurich. The date of operation was I April 1912 and even the reputedly dour Swiss have a sense of humour, I suspect." [Tramfare] "The illustrations are well reproduced and include some fascinating, animated views from the impressive but seldom-illustrated collection of Pam Eaton. This book endeavours to be a complete survey of overseas double-deck electric cars and necessarily only an overview of other means of propulsion, but it is unlikely ever to superseded except by an updated edition by the same author. It well merits a place on the bookshelf of any tramway student with a catholic interest in this form of design. [Tramways & Urban Transit]

## The Twilight Years of the Edinburgh Tram

**Alan Brotchie. Softback, A4, 194 photographs, including 152 in colour, 112pp, £25.**

"...the author has done well to assemble so many views in colour ... the book is a worthy reminder of a fine tramway system that should never have been destroyed." [Tramway Review]

"...the descriptive captions are highly appropriate, and provide a neat yet clear and comprehensive overview of the system's closing years ... the quality of both content and production are sufficient advertisement." [TMS Journal]

## The Twilight Years of the Trams in Aberdeen and Dundee

**Softback, 120pp, 231 illustrations, mostly coloured, with captions and Introduction by Alan Brotchie, £25**

## The Twilight Years of the Glasgow Tram

**Softback, 144 pages, £25.**

Contains over 250 coloured pictures taken by Douglas McMillan, selected, prefaced and captioned by Alasdair Turnbull, who has maintained a humorous and homely commentary on a clockwise tour of the Glasgow system as it was in the 1950's and early 1960's. Published to celebrate the centenary of the introduction of electric traction to the Glasgow tramways on 13th October 1898.

"Every so often one comes across a book which is almost beyond compare, and this is one such. More, it is sure to set a new standard for albums, and one to which every author and publisher might do well to aspire…a wonderful book…" [Tramway Museum Society Journal]

## Glasgow Subway Album

**George Watson. Softback, A4, 64pp, all colour, £10.**

"The pictures reflect the day to day life on the line and as such proves to be a superb record of the only other subway line in the UK other than London Transport. With 115 colour pictures the volume is excellent value." [Tramfare]

"What is amazing about this volume is the quality of the photographs, for almost all were taken under artificial lighting, in large spaces where the use of flash lighting would be wholly ineffective, yet the colour is mostly quite natural, portraying the system much as the human eye would see it. For this the publisher and his printer must also be congratulated ... this is a superb production covering a little-known railway, and does its job very well indeed." [TMS Journal]

## Tramways and Electric Railways in the Nineteenth Century

**(Electric Railway Number of Cassier's Magazine, 1899), cloth hardback, over 250pp, £23**

## Toy and Model Trams of the World, Volume 1

**Gottfried Kure and David Voice, 128pp, A4, all colour, £25.**

[Back cover comment]: "Following a lifetime of modelling and collecting small trams (the authors) have teamed up to pool their knowledge in this definitive work describing toy and model trams, trolleybuses and underground trains from over the whole world. In volume I the authors look at toy trams, all die cast small trams and the vast souvenir market. The book gives invaluable tips about collecting and looking after toy trams, then covers historical tinplate, tinplate after 1950, wood, card, die cast, plastic, all other materials, souvenirs and children's toys. To help identify items there is a manufacturers' index and around 400 illustrations, mainly full colour photographs. Over 1,800 individual small trams, trolleybuses and underground trains are included and there are around 480 manufacturers' names, most entries having an historical summary. The book also guides the collector with market price estimates for toy trams no longer in production."

## Toy and Model Trams of the World, Volume 2

**Plastic, White Metal and Brass Models and Kits. Gottfied Kure and David Voice, A4 softback, 188pp, £30.**

[Back cover comment]: "Once again Gottfried Kuře and David Voice have teamed up to pool their knowledge in this definitive work describing models and kits of trams, trolleybuses, underground trains, funiculars and monorails from all over the world. Volume 2 takes the story from Volume 1 and looks at the vast range of models and kits that have been produced from countries all over the world. The introduction looks at the various scales and gauges in use, then the three main manufacturing materials: plastic, white metal and brass. The final chapter looks back to Volume 1 and adds new information that has come to light since its publication. To help identify models the book contains an index of manufacturers for both volumes and there are around 600 full colour photographs. Around 4,000 individual model trams and kits are identified, with the listing in each chapter being alphabetical by manufacturer. There are around 1,000 manufacturers named, most having a historical summary."

## The Wantage Tramway

**S.H. Pearce Higgins, reprint of 1958 publication, hardback, green cloth, dust wrapper, 158pp + illustrations, £28**

## Clippie

**Z.Katin, a few months in the life of a tram and bus conductress in the war in Sheffield, 124pp, softback, reprint, £7**

"When I was married, at the age of 22, I tried for a long time to obtain work. At the end of 18 years' interrupted effort I succeeded. The second world war had made its debut just as I had resigned myself to the knowledge that in Britain a married woman may not work outside her home except as a charlady.

Soon after my husband was called up and my son had turned 14 there came a request from the Minister of Labour and National Service that I call at the employment exchange and there be directed to work of national importance. I was not thrilled. My desire to help in the war effort was tinged with a resentment that society could only find work for me in a period of destruction and sudden death, and then only by resorting to organised compulsion.

At the "Labour" they told me I was a year too young to be given clerical work. "Could I join the Land Army?" I asked. Yes, I could, but I must be prepared to leave home. "That won't do, because my son is still at school." Very well, as you are a non-mobile woman, you have two alternatives left:

You can go into a factory; or
You can go into transport.

I thought of the heat, noise, electric light and airlessness of a munition factory and then I thought of the fresh air that blows from the Yorkshire moors across a tramcar platform in my city. And so I became a clippie – a tram conductress.

## The Wearing of the Green

**William Tollan. Softback, A4 size, 96 pages, 64 pages in mono, 16 pages in colour; covers coloured on both sides, £12**

This describes the Glasgow tramways from c.1928-1951 from the viewpoint of a driver and conductor. "I think this is the most fascinating and amusing book on trams I have ever read." [Publisher]

"This is a dangerous book. Dangerous because once you pick it up you will find it impossible to put down until the end! ... Excellent value for money and thoroughly recommended." [Industrial Heritage]

"The book recalls the day when the tram reigned supreme over most of Clydesdale; it is well illustrated and appendices include extracts from traffic circulars and a full list of fare stages and a glossary. You will enjoy this book and even find the English translation of Auchenshuggle. [Tramway Review]

Titles may be ordered from bookshops, or direct from the publisher at the address below. Postage and packing on new books, UK retail: please add 10% of the value of the order up to £4.90 maximum. Orders £50 and over post free. Overseas orders, postage extra at cost, please specify surface or airmail. Overseas payments must please be by cheque, drawn on a British bank, payable in sterling.

**ADAM GORDON, Kintradwell Farmhouse, Brora, Sutherland, KW9 6LU. Tel: 01408 622660.**